W9-BFM-212

PROPERTY
TOWN OF OXFORD

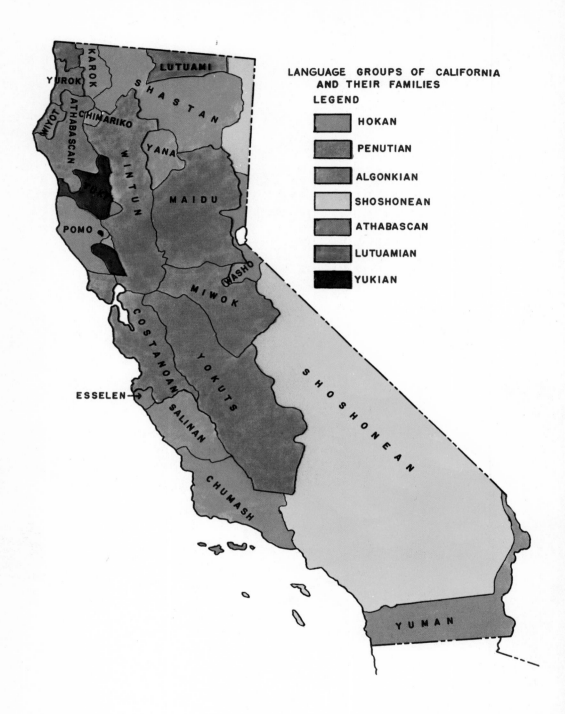

LANGUAGE GROUPS OF CALIFORNIA
AND THEIR FAMILIES
LEGEND

HOKAN
PENUTIAN
ALGONKIAN
SHOSHONEAN
ATHABASCAN
LUTUAMIAN
YUKIAN

KAROK

YUROK

WIYOT

ATHABASCAN

CHIMARIKO

LUTUAMI

SHASTAN

YANA

YUKI

WINTUN

MAIDU

POMO

WASHO

MIWOK

COSTANOAM

ESSELEN →

YOKUTS

SALINAN

CHUMASH

SHOSHONEAN

YUMAN

SEVEN MAIN LANGUAGE GROUPS*

1) ATHABASCAN: (*North*)   Tolowa, Hupa, Chilula, Whilkut, Mattole, Nongatl, Sinkyone, Lassik, Kato, Wailaki

2) ALGONKIN: (*North*)   Yurok, Wiyot

3) YUKIAN: (*North*)   Yuki (and Coast Yuki), Huchnon, Wappo

4) LUTAMIAN: (*North*)   Modoc (related to Klamath Indians of Oregon)

5) HOKAN: (*North and Central*)   Shastan (Achomawi, Atsugewi—Pit River)
Yana (north-central)
Yahi (Deer and Mill Creeks)
Karok (Salmon River)
Chimariko (Trinity River)
Pomo (north coast)
Washo (Lake Tahoe)
Esselen (central coast)
Salinan (Salinas Valley)
Chumash (Santa Barbara, Ventura)
Yuman: Yuma, Mohave Desert areas and Diegueño (San Diego)

6) PENUTIAN: (*Central and South*)   Wintun (Sacramento Valley)
Maidu (northeast border)
Miwok (Sierra Nevada Mountains)
Costonoan (San Francisco area)
Yokuts (San Joaquin Valley)

7) SHOSHONEAN: (*South*)   PLATEAU BRANCH—

     MONO-BANNOCK GROUP: (Death Valley and south)
       North Paiute
       Mono

     SHOSHONE-COMANCHE GROUP: (Death Valley)
       Panamint (or Koso)

     UTE-CHEMEHUEVI GROUP: (south of Death Valley)
       Chemehuevi (or South Paiute)
       Kawaiisu

   KERN RIVER BRANCH—(Kern River)
     Tubatulabal

  SOUTHERN CALIFORNIA BRANCH—(Mt. Baldy and Mt. San Gorgonio)
     SERRANO GROUP: Alliklik, Vanyune, Serrano
     GABRIELEÑO GROUP: Gabrieleño (Los Angeles area)
     LUISEÑO-CAHUILLA GROUP: Juaneño, Luiseño, Cupeño (San Diego and Palm Springs)

* See Also: Maps of tribes Pages 133 and 135, and Chart of tribes, locations, and main differences Pages 140–157

by Helen Bauer

CALIFORNIA INDIAN DAYS

Helen Bauer

LINE DRAWINGS BY DON FREEMAN

DOUBLEDAY & COMPANY, INC.
GARDEN CITY, NEW YORK

TO
the Logermans,
Roberta Jean and Calvin
and
their children,
Lynn Ann and Gail Ellen

970.4
B

4816

Library of Congress Catalog Card Number 63–7571
Copyright © 1963 by Helen Bauer
All Rights Reserved
Printed in the United States of America

ACKNOWLEDGMENTS

THE AUTHOR wishes to give respectful acknowledgment to all authoritative sources of material on the subject of California Indians. The books from which I have reaped the facts presented in my book have been many and I hereby express sincere gratitude and a sense of obligation for all such help.

There are many who have furnished the important pictorial material contained therein. To all of them I give due credit and genuine appreciation. Among them are: Arthur Barr, president, Arthur Barr Productions, Inc., for permission to use the photographs of Indian life and who has furnished me with photographs for my other three California books; Hubert A. Lowman, my good friend, whose photographs have been used in all of my books; Campbell Grant, artist and authority on pictographs, Trustee of the Santa Barbara Museum of Natural History; Dr. Charles Rozaire, formerly of Southwest Museum, Los Angeles, now of Nevada State Museum, Carson City, whose mother has been my lifelong friend; Karl Obert (photographs furnished by the California Conservation Council, Santa Barbara); Robert C. Frampton Photos, Claremont (assisted by my son, Dr. Sherwin Carlquist, Associate Professor of Botany, Claremont Graduate School, Claremont Colleges and Rancho Santa Ana Botanic Garden, Claremont); R. M. Ariss, Department of Anthropology, Los Angeles County Museum; Robert H. Lowie Museum of Anthropology, University of California, Berkeley; the Museum of Natural History of Santa Barbara for permission to allow Bosworth Lemere, Carpenteria, to take photographs of the exhibits in the museum; the U. S. Forest Service (San Francisco); California Div. of Forestry (San Francisco); Division of Mines, State of California (San Francisco) for the relief maps; and the U. S. Bureau of Reclamation (Sacramento). Especial appreciation is due to Dr. Paul D. Scherer, Associate Professor of Industrial Arts, University of California, Santa Barbara, for making possible the production of the maps in the book.

Praise, appreciation and a full measure of credit goes to Don Freeman of Santa Barbara, a well-known and skillful artist, who is responsible for the artwork at the beginning of each chapter. The collaboration with him in the coordination of text and artwork has been a rewarding experience. His wife, Lydia Freeman, deserves and is hereby given a generous share of gratitude for her painstaking and carefully executed artwork.

I offer my heartfelt appreciation to my many understanding friends who remained my true and loyal friends during the time I was "out of circulation" during the writing of this book.

A genuine expression of gratitude is due and hereby given to the able members of the editorial staff of the publisher for their ever-present understanding, patience, and friendly guidance.

One may spend endless hours in concentrated effort, but must also rely on the assistance and encouragement of family members. In particular, I acknowledge the help, faith, and patience of my husband, Roy M. Bauer. A rightful and full measure of credit is given to my son, Dr. Sherwin Carlquist, the constant guide, critic, and motivator of my writing and whose efforts were particularly helpful in the planning and securing of written and pictorial material on the subject of plants used by the Indians of that early time.

CONTENTS

PREFACE

CALIFORNIA's story really began many thousands of years ago. Before any other peoples lived here, Indians roamed the oak-studded valleys and foothills; built their huts upon the river banks; lived along the beautiful coast and on the barren deserts. It is believed that there were about one hundred fifty thousand of them, more than in any other part of North America. They took food from the places they lived, as well as materials for their homes and all other things needed to meet the demands of their simple way of life. Not all the Indian groups throughout the state had the same customs and the story told here will not be right for all tribes. However, there is a chart at the end of the book that points out some of the main differences between the family groups.

The story of the Indians is an interesting but sad one. Once Indians owned everything they could see from their villages. You will want to read about the changes that came and what happened to these early-day Californians who began the first period in the history of California. Much of the period is only a dim memory. Place names, stone mortars and tools, painted rocks, stories told by early explorers and pioneers—these are all that remain as a record of that time. We wish that we knew more about these people. As time goes on and places are found where Indians once lived, the story will be somewhat more complete. Parts of it may never be known, only imagined. It is hoped that those who read this book will gain an appreciation for and an understanding of the California Indians who lived here and called it their home.

Polar map showing close relation of Asia and North America. The people of Asia moved across the narrow strip of water and islands into North America.

1 CALIFORNIA BEGINNINGS

Many moons ago in the faraway beginning years, California was a land of Indians. How and when they came to California no one really knows. There is no record to tell us; nothing was written, only remembered. Those who have studied about such things believe that the Indians came from Asia. They must have come to this continent long before there were boats that could cross an ocean. The only place they could have reached North America was by way of Alaska across the Bering Strait. (see map) At this point, Siberia and Alaska are about sixty miles apart. In between the two places are stepping-stone islands, the Diomedes. The longest distance between these islands is only about twenty-five miles. When the Bering Strait is frozen over, it can be crossed on the ice. The first people to come to this continent may have found a way over these icy areas. It is known also that this area was once dry land and they could have walked across from Siberia to Alaska. Whatever way they came or why they came is still a mystery.

The one fact known is that they came a very long time ago and over a period of many thousands of years. Scientists believe that Indians lived in central California about forty-five hundred years ago and in the northwestern part, about two thousand years ago. Along the southern coast, the desert areas, and west of the Sierra Nevada Mountains, they think that some Indians came about ten thousand years ago.

Scientists guess that the Indians went southward from Alaska to Canada. At that time Canada was also a land covered with ice and snow. For several thousand years there was an ice-free avenue in Canada and south of Canada along the Rocky Mountains. Some of the Indians followed the Rocky Mountains down to the lower Colorado River area and then went west to California. Some groups wandered to the east and still others went further and further south and some went to the southernmost tip of South America. (see map)

No one knows exactly how many Indians settled in California. Some think that there may have been as many as 130,-000 to 150,000 of them. If this is true, there were more Indians in California than in any other part of the United States. Some think that there were more Indians in the Santa Barbara area, especially on the Santa Barbara Islands, than in any other place in California.

The Indians who stayed in California found it to be a good land, a place where they could build their simple homes and hunt and fish. The climate was warmer than in other places they had been and there was plenty of food. Wherever Indians settled in California, in the valleys, on the hills, or in the mountains, they believed that the new land belonged to them and that it always would.

For thousands of years these people lived and worked with only crude tools of bone, stone, and shell. There were neither horses nor cattle. No one taught them how to sew or cook, plant

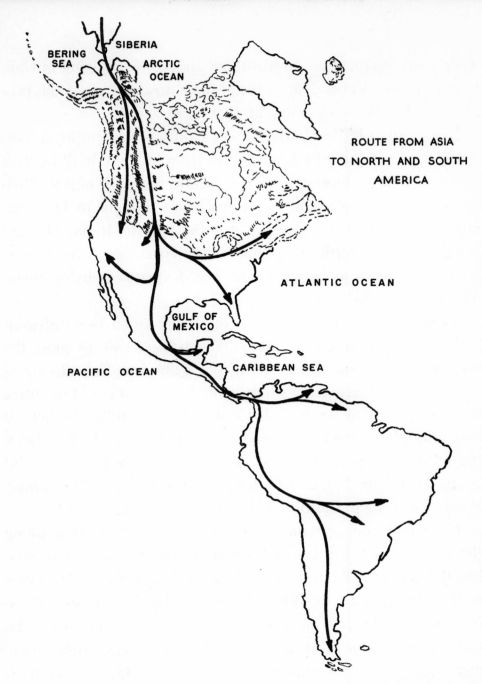

ROUTE FROM ASIA
TO NORTH AND SOUTH
AMERICA

or build. Nature and a little work took care of their daily needs. In those early years when California was young, the Indians felt happy and free from danger. Then in 1542 came another people, pale of skin unlike their own. Perhaps the brown-skinned people wanted to say to them, "Go! Leave us in peace!" These strangers to California's shores were explorers sent by Spain.

They were the first ones to learn that Indians were living in California. Their records give us the earliest descriptions of the people and the life they lived at that time.

It was June of 1542 when Juan Rodríguez Cabrillo, a Portuguese explorer sent by Spain, sailed from Mexico. In those days maps were very poor but Cabrillo hoped to find a passage through or around unknown land (California was thought to be an island) that would prove to be a short way to India. He had been told, "Sail north along the western coast. See if the land is fertile and green along the shore. See if anyone is living there. Try to find good harbors."

At times the wind beat back the white-sailed *San Salvador* and the smaller ship, *La Victoria*. When there was no wind, the ships bobbed about like corks in the quiet sea. Cabrillo could only wonder where the winds would carry them. For three months he headed northward. He watched carefully but saw no way through the land but one day he found an open place along the shore. He and his men guided the ships toward it and found it to be a "good and safe harbor" (present-day San Diego Bay). Even then Cabrillo did not know where he was.

The sailors could see dark-skinned people running about along the shore. When they landed they found only a few Indians who had not run away from the strangers. Cabrillo held out his hands with palms upward to show that he and his men wished to be friendly. After a few days some of the Indians came back. To them Cabrillo gave beads and small gifts. How very strange these men with white skins must have looked to the Indians! Perhaps they thought of them as gods from the "spirit world." The ships sailed on but before he left, Cabrillo had given the name of San Miguel to the "safe harbor."

The weather was good and the wind right. The ships sailed northward again and anchored at an island we now know as Santa Catalina. Here the Indians were friendly. Leaving the is-

Indians thought that this beautiful new land belonged to them. (Karl Obert)

land, Cabrillo kept close to the coast. He noted the pleasant country with its valleys, plains, and mountains. Coming close to the land, his men saw smoke from many fires. The ships anchored near the shore where many small villages could be seen. Cabrillo named the place the Bay of Smokes (*Bahia de las Fumas*). It is believed that this was present-day San Pedro Bay.

The two ships continued sailing along the coast. Near what is now called Ventura, canoes paddled by Indians darted out through the waves to meet the strange ships with white wings. Cabrillo thought a good name for this place would be the Town of Boats (*el Pueblo de Canoas*). The sailors visited the villages along the shore and the white men and the Indians gave gifts to each other. At a point near Point Mugu (Ventura County), Cabrillo raised the flag of Spain, on October 10, 1542. From that day on, California was supposed to belong to Spain.

Records from that time show that Cabrillo's ships stopped at several places along the Santa Barbara coast. One place was Dos Pueblos (Two Towns) where there were two Indian villages (*rancherías,* the Spanish called them). Between the villages was a small stream. Indians on one side of the stream did not look like nor speak the same language as those on the other side. Those in one village were short and fat and those in the other were thin and taller and their skins were a lighter color.

Heavy winds forced the ships out to sea. They found shelter in a snug harbor on San Miguel, one of the Santa Barbara Islands. Here again the explorers were received with kindness. On this island Cabrillo fell and broke his arm. However, he had no thought of turning back and so he ordered his men to sail on toward the north. They ran into storms and rough seas and there was no land in sight. Then Cabrillo saw a curve of land like a bay (Monterey Bay). It looked like a good harbor but he could not find out because of the stormy weather. There seemed to be nothing to do but turn back to the island near the Santa Barbara coast. All this time Cabrillo's arm had been getting worse. He fell ill and died while his ships were in the island harbor. The sailors buried the brave Cabrillo on the island of San Miguel. Before he died Cabrillo had told his pilot, Bartolomé Ferrelo, "Go on and on. Do what I was not able to do." Ferrelo and his men sailed as far north as Oregon. No way was found through the land. No "cities of gold," as told about in old stories, were found by the men. So the ships turned homeward again. Cabrillo and his men had not discovered a short cut to India but they did find out many things not known before about that part of the world. Their journey had taken them all the way up the coast of South America and eight hundred miles of the Pacific Coast. Now they knew that there was a mainland, not

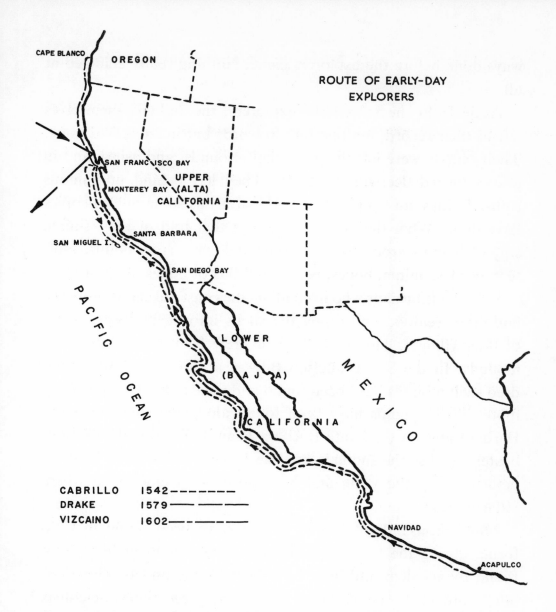

CAPE BLANCO OREGON

SAN FRANCISCO BAY
UPPER
MONTEREY BAY (ALTA)
CALIFORNIA

SANTA BARBARA
SAN MIGUEL I.
SAN DIEGO BAY

PACIFIC

OCEAN

L O W E R

(B A J A)

C A L I F O R N I A

M E X I C O

NAVIDAD

ACAPULCO

CABRILLO 1542 – – – – – –
DRAKE 1579 —— — ——
VIZCAINO 1602 —– - —– —

just one large island or a group of small islands through which ships could pass. They brought back news about the beautiful land they had seen and about the Indians living there.

For almost fifty years after Cabrillo's voyage, other explorers came from countries in the Old World. Their records also tell about the Indians living in California. The last explorer who came during those early years was Sebastian Vizcaíno, in 1602. Then, strange as it seems, California was forgotten for more than a hundred and sixty years. The Indians lived on as they had always done before the explorers came. Nothing really changed at all.

Aside from the records of explorers, the Indians themselves left us their record, not one told in words but in stone and bone. Their secrets were left in caves, shell mounds, and ashes, and in graves buried deep in the earth. They left behind no famous ruins of cities, no temples nor works of art as some other peoples have done. What they left were things that told of their simple way of living—crude tools of chipped stone, arrow points, mortars, pestles, animal bones, beads, and bits of bones in old graves.

Early Californians who lived along the coast ate clams, mussels, and other seafood and threw the shells into heaps by the sides of their villages. The piles of shells grew from heaps into great mounds. In the San Francisco Bay area alone, over four hundred such mounds have been found and once there were probably more. Shell mounds have been found along the shore in Santa Barbara and on the Santa Barbara Islands. Wind and rain have beaten against the mounds but the broken shells have held together during the years and have given us a clue as to where villages once stood.

Many thousands of Indian objects have been found in California during the last hundred years. Many of them have been found by accident and have been kept by the finders. However, others are in museums where visitors may see them. Scientists spend their lives in search of these objects. Every year more and more of them are found. In this way, bit by bit, pieces of the puzzle can be put together to help us understand the life of that time. In 1961 at the Arlington Springs Site on Santa Rosa Island, for example, a man's bone was found that proved to be ten thousand years old. Before that no one believed that Indians had lived in California so long ago. By this kind of careful study, scientists are gradually reaching further and further back into the past.

Besides the records of early explorers and the Indian objects that have been found, we have still another clue as to the people and customs of that long-ago time. There are Indians still living in California who remember stories of early days told to them by their parents and grandparents. These stories had been passed on from their parents and grandparents before that and so on down from age to age and tribe to tribe, through many hundreds of years. As time goes on, it is hoped that we will know even more than we do now about early Indian days. We are fortunate to know as much as we do about these first Californians.

Indians left their secrets buried deep in the earth. (Exhibit, Santa Barbara Museum of Natural History)

2 TRIBES AND VILLAGES

Even though there were many thousands of Indians in California, the state is so large that they could not have lived in all parts of it. Wherever they lived, however, they must have loved their beautiful California home. There were towering mountains, some snow-covered most of the year. High-set valleys had great stony cliffs around them. Lower valleys were green or sometimes brown, and in spring there were wide carpets of blue, purple, and gold-colored flowers. There were fish in the rushing rivers and quiet lakes and wild animals in the forests. Trees and bushes were heavy with acorns, seeds, nuts, fruits, and berries. West of the mountains was a very long shoreline. Here waves lapped and foamed against rocks or rolled up on the sandy beaches. Beyond the mountains to the east were wide desert places.

Indians who lived in one part of California and who spoke the same language were called a tribe. Actually the word "tribe" meant very little to them. If asked, they might not have been able to tell to which group or tribe they belonged. In those very

There were high towering mountains, some snow-covered most of the year.
(Karl Obert)

early years, they all seemed to belong to one people with many families.

So far as we know, there were more languages spoken by the California Indians than by any other group in the United States. At one time there were twenty-one language groups, with seven main divisions.* Besides these main language groups there were 135 dialects, or ways of speaking the same language. Today it is said that many Americans only use about five hundred words. California Indians used many more than that and most of the words had many different shades of meaning.

* *See map, frontispiece.*

Usually these groups belonged to a village or villages or lived on certain pieces of land they thought of as their own. In most cases the group was divided into several villages or settlements, each having families related to one another. In some areas there was one large village and several smaller ones. People in the smaller villages could move about from place to place and live where they wished in their own territory. Those who lived in the important main village could not move to other places. Nearly every group had a chief or headman and he lived in the main village. A smaller village had a lesser chief.

The cluster of houses that made up a village clung to main rivers or branches of them. Usually the larger villages were near the larger streams. Some villages were in the wide open canyons.

Wild animals were in the forest. (Karl Obert)

Indians lived along the seacoast, by lakes, along main rivers and their branches.

Permanent houses were not built high in the mountains or on the rolling hills. Wherever the village, a water supply had to be nearby. Desert Indians lived near springs of water. Groups left their homes in different seasons to gather various foods as they

They lived along the rivers. (U. S. Bureau of Reclamation)

ripened. Usually the headman of the village led his people to the food-gathering places each year.

Some of the villages had only a few families; some had hundreds. Some tribes had to have a larger territory. The Canaliño villages, for example, were many and were scattered along the coast from the Los Angeles area to San Luis Obispo and on the Santa Barbara Islands. Around Goleta there were twenty-five to thirty villages. An explorer's journal said that there were about one hundred houses and a thousand people living near Santa Barbara (near the entrance to the present-day University of California, Santa Barbara). Dos Pueblos (on the Santa Barbara coast), with its two villages had about a thousand people. It was reported that there was a cluster of five other Chumash villages in which there were several thousand Indians living.

The Yokuts of San Joaquin Valley had a larger tribe and spoke a language that was unlike any other. Their territory was larger than any of those in the north. Their villages were small and there were many of them. The Shoshonean tribe was about the size of the Yokuts but they had the largest territory in California. (see color map in front of book)

3 WHAT WERE THESE INDIANS LIKE?

THE Indians varied in their looks just as they did in their customs and languages. Most of them had wide faces and broad noses. Most of them were short and of heavy build. Some had narrow heads with thin faces and were tall. People of the Yuki tribe were short, had narrow heads and broad noses. The Mohaves in the south had broad heads but were a tall people.

Some of the tribes were dark-skinned, almost black. These were the ones who lived near the ocean or in warmer places. Many were no darker than a light tan. It is known that all of them had dark brown eyes.

All of the Indians had straight black hair. Usually it grew low on the forehead. Almost all of them wore their hair long. Men tied it up at the back of the head and stuck a hunting knife in the knot. What a handy place for that! Canaliño women wore their hair cut in bangs across the front. They took great pride in the long hair that hung over their shoulders. Sometimes bands of shells were worn around the head like a flat crown. Thin, bone hairpins have been found and so we know that some women used them. Hair was brushed with a little bundle of stiff fibers. Some of the women mixed mesquite gum with clay and left it on their hair for a few days. When washed, the hair was clean and shiny. Young women and girls may have tucked flowers into their hair in order to make them look pretty.

Some have thought that California Indians lived in a very poor way, worked very little, and had few arts and crafts. Others who have studied about them have found that this is not quite true. Some of the groups had great skill in making baskets. Not much pottery was made but it was designed rather well. The Chumash men built boats that were better than any others built by Indian tribes in the United States. Beautiful ornaments were made by coastal Indians and traded to inland tribes. Bowls, pipes, and other soapstone (steatite) articles were of good design and polish. Some were inlaid with bits of shiny shells. Other articles that proved their skills were the mortars, pestles, arrow points,

Fiber hairbrush.

Women wore ornaments even when they went food-gathering. (Los Angeles County Museum)

It is surprising to learn that these early-day people made objects so well (steatite bowl, steatite boat-shape charm, steatite whale charm, bone harpoon point, bone fish hook, stone knife). (Southwest Museum, Los Angeles)

and all kinds of useful things made by patient work. It is surprising to learn that these early-day people made as many objects as they did with no tools to help them.

The first white settlers who came to California called the Indians "Digger" Indians. They saw women digging in the earth day after day. Their main way of life was to gather food and some-

Exhibit shows use of mortar and pestle, metate and mano, and cooking with hot stones. (Santa Barbara Museum of Natural History)

times the food was underground. Women used sticks to dig up roots that were used for food. They dug for roots used in making their baskets and they helped dig out the ground for their homes. So, it is true that they did dig, but no tribe was ever called "Digger" even though that name is sometimes still given to California Indians.

Many think of Indians as being warriors. For hundreds of years most of the California Indians lived in peace with each other. When the explorers found them, they were probably a happy, contented people most of the time. They were slow to anger. War was usually for the "fun of the game" or for some gain. At that time their only enemies were other Indian tribes that came into their territory to take food. Each tribe had its own area and no other tribe or family was allowed to take food from another unless told that he could do so. If a tribe had more than could be used by its members, it was glad to trade with those of other tribes. Their needs were simple, however, and each day they lived with what they had.

Southern California Indian woman making acorn meal. (Exhibit, Los Angeles County Museum)

4 DEERSKINS AND NECKLACES

CLOTHING worn by the Indians was very simple and varied with the climate and season. If hot, they wore less; if cold they wore more. Usually little clothing was worn and little needed. In the warm summer months the men wore nothing at all or just a skin folded about their hips. What they lacked in clothing, they made up for by decorating their faces and bodies. This was done by painting red, black, and white designs in figures and stripes. White paint was supposed to fool the "evil spirits" and scare them away.

Paints could be washed off but not the tattoo designs, which were made by pricking the skin with cactus spines or something sharp. Dyes or black soot from the fire were rubbed into the designs pricked on the skin. Women liked tattoos even more than the men. They believed that the deep-blue dots and lines made them beautiful.

Women wore a short skirt in two pieces, the narrow, smaller one worn in the front. A larger but shorter piece came around

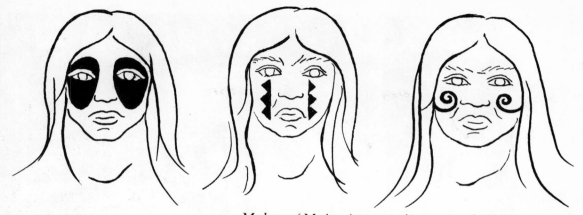

Mohave (Mojave) men—face paint designs.

the hips to meet the front skirt or apron. Skirts were made of deerskin or other animal skins or from fibers. The bottom half of a skin skirt was slit into strips or fringes. Such skirts made for ease in walking or sitting at work. Fiber skirts were made from the inner bark of trees or tule, shredded and gathered together on a fiber cord. Women liked to decorate the ends of the fringes with bits of tar, tiny shells, or even pine nuts. Some women dyed the skirts a bright red.

Men as well as women liked to wear ornaments. Men's necklaces were of birds' beaks, animal teeth, or large shells. Ear ornaments were rods about the size of a small finger, made of wood, bone, shell, or an animal's tooth. These were put through a hole in the ear.

Indian women were especially fond of ornaments and beads of all kinds. The favorite ones were strings of many-colored shells, or of bits of soapstone and bone. Beads with very fine carvings

Mohave (Mojave) women—face paint designs.

Fringed skirts made it easier to sit while working. (Arthur Barr Productions, Inc.)

on them have been found. Some strings of beads were so long that they hung to the waist and many of them had ornaments on the ends. Strings of shells were worn around the wrists also. Hairbands and belts were made of brightly-colored birds' feathers and bits of shells.

Most people wear caps or hats to protect them from the sun. Not so the Indian women. For them, the pretty little tightly-woven caps had another important use. Theirs were to protect their foreheads when carrying heavy burden baskets in their nets when they went out food-gathering. Some of the caps were coiled and some twined just like the baskets made in various areas. (see chapter 9) Some had woodpecker feathers or blue quail feathers woven into them. Usually the caps were made round to fit the head. The Shoshonean women wore peaked ones while others made flatter shaped caps.

Young children wore no clothes at all. Older girls wore skirts like their mothers. Young boys wore the same kind of skins around their hips as their fathers did.

Moccasins of skin, tule, or yucca fiber were their shoes. Everyone went barefooted around the village. Moccasins were worn only on wood-gathering or food-gathering trips or perhaps in cold weather. When father took out his moccasins, the family knew that he was going on a hunting trip of some kind. Northern California Indians wore a one-piece, unsoled soft shoe. The sock-like deerskin moccasin had one seam up the front, and another up the heel (Hurok, Miwok, Hupa, Modoc style). The front seam was puckered up the front. The heel was made by drawing a leather thong through it. Tribes of southern California

Ornaments of shell and bone. (Santa Barbara Museum of Natural History)

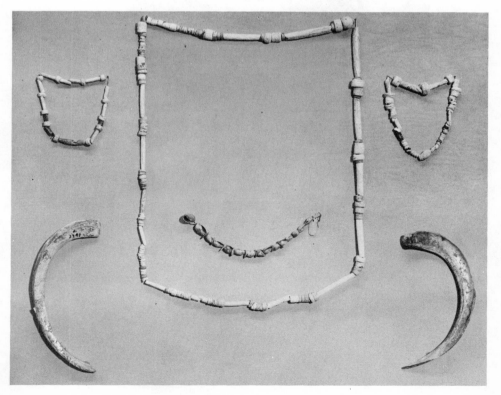

Women wore caps to protect their foreheads when carrying burden baskets. (Santa Barbara Museum of Natural History)

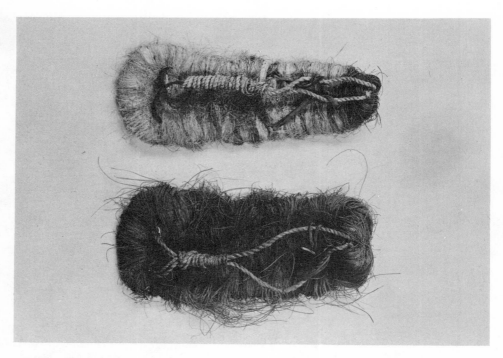

Fiber moccasins. (Robert H. Lowie, Museum of Anthropology, University of California, Berkeley)

wore sandals of woven fibers wrapped around a looped frame. The sole was an inch thick. Hot, sun-dried earth could not be felt through these.

Leggings or high moccasins woven of tule fibers were used in some parts of northern California. Leggings for snowy weather were probably made of some kind of animal skin. Layers of soft grass in the bottom of them made walking easier and kept feet warmer.

When the weather was cold, rainy, or windy, more clothing was needed. Men, women, and children had deerskin blankets that they threw over their shoulders like a cape. Some wrapped the blanket around the body, over one arm and under the other and tied it in front. Soft sea otter fur was best to use but it was not so easy to get. Another kind of blanket was made of woven strips of rabbit fur. Such a blanket was worn in the daytime and used as a cover at night. Some records show that Indians covered their bodies with mud to keep warm in the colder months.

Pendants of various sizes and materials were worn on necklaces. (Southwest Museum, Los Angeles)

5 HOUSES OF TULE, BRUSH, AND BARK

INDIANS built houses which would seem very strange to us. Houses had to be built with whatever material they could find and in ways that would fit their needs. There were no saws to cut down trees and nothing but stone tools to make planks.

Most of the Indians lived outdoors a good deal of the time; houses were used more for sleeping than anything else. In some areas the weather was very hot, while in parts of the north the weather was cold for several months of the year. Some houses were made of tule, some were made of rough bark planks, and still others were covered with earth. In desert areas the houses were little more than shelters from the hot sun. Some of the houses were large enough for several families; others were very small. Some were shaped like a dome, some like a cone, and some had a ridge-style roof. Notched ladders were used to climb into some of the houses. Others had doors so low that the Indians had to crawl to get into them.

In the north where the Yurok and Hupa families lived, the winters were wet and cold. There were forests of oaks and pines in their area and so their houses were of tree bark planks. The planks were split with a strong elkhorn wedge. If a fallen tree was found in the forest, this was used. If not, the tree had to be burned down by a fire set at the base. The Shasta family, also in the north, had much the same type of house except that a deep hole was dug and a plank roof placed over the top of it. This cellar-like house was cozy and warm in the winter months.

In the center of the floor in these houses there was a small hole where the fire was made. Above the fire, one of the planks was raised to let the smoke out. Here during the long winter months the mother cooked the food and the family ate and worked. At night the children slept there with their mother. Father went to another place to sleep called the sweat house.

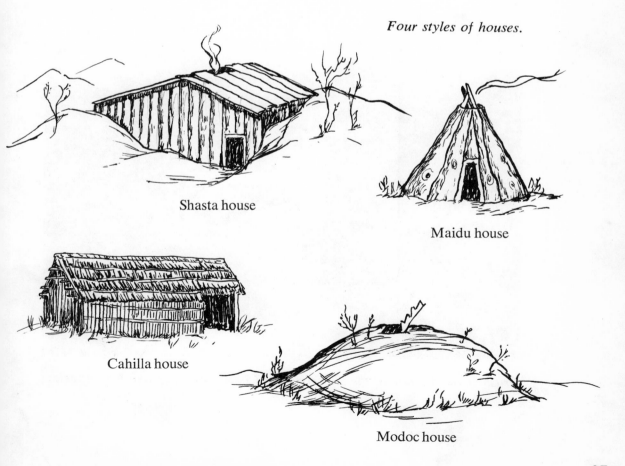

Four styles of houses.

Shasta house

Maidu house

Cahilla house

Modoc house

Tribes to the south and east also had tree bark houses. Theirs were cone-shaped and not so well-made. The Sacramento Valley houses were mostly under the ground. Above the ground, the house was cone-shaped and covered with brush, not planks.

Many tribes such as the Chumash and the Yokuts had round, dome-like brush houses. First, men set poles into the ground in a circle. Inside the circle of poles a hole about two feet deep was dug. The tops of the poles were then bent together and tied with strips of leather or willow bark. Smaller poles were tied crossways around the sides of the house. Women and children went to nearby marshes and gathered armloads of tule reed. The tule reed was woven into mats and fastened to the sides of the little house. An opening was left at the top to let in a little light and fresh air. A fire in the middle of the house kept everyone warm on cool nights. Wisps of smoke floated out through

Brush-covered house of the Shoshoneans. (Southwest Museum, Los Angeles)

The tule bed was covered with a skin blanket. (Arthur Barr Productions, Inc.)

the hole left in the center of the roof. There was a small door on one side of the house, with a mat hung over it to keep out wind, cold, or rain. The extra dirt dug from the hole was put around the outside base of the house. This helped to keep the house warm and dry. In some areas where the weather was colder, the same kind of house was built except that mud was put over the tule mats or brush.

The beds the Indians used were probably not very comfortable. The Yokuts made beds by digging a hole in the dirt floor and filling it with dried tule grass. Some families spread tule mats on the floor near the center fire. Others piled mats around the inside walls and slept on them. Sometimes springy pine needles were placed under the mats to make the beds softer.

Clothes, storage baskets and other things, they owned and used were hung around the sides of the walls or on shelves dug into the earth. Think of how crowded these small houses must have been! In the evening by the warm, cozy fire, the family sang and listened to stories told by the older ones.

Most families had several small houses. They moved about in their own territory looking for food. Food-gathering times in summer and fall were like vacations. When they went up into the hills or mountains they gathered enough seeds and acorns to last until the next season. In each place they stayed awhile, they put up a light brush-covered shelter, open at the sides and held up by four poles.

There was another kind of house in many villages called a *temescal* or sweat house. It was given this name because it was

Small house or sweat house of the Luiseño tribe. (Southwest Museum, Los Angeles)

so warm inside that Indians could sweat freely. Only California tribes had such sweat houses. The Colorado Indians and some of the desert tribes were hot enough without that kind of house!

Tribes having such sweat houses used them daily in several ways. The *temescal* was something like a men's smoking and sleeping club. Here the men met to sit, smoke, talk, sing, tell stories, or play games. Men slept in them at night. Women did not go to the sweat houses except on very special occasions.

The sweat house was used as a place for curing the sick also. A very hot fire was made in the center of the room. Since there was no smoke hole, the sweat house became hot and smoky. Men lay on the floor and stayed there as long as they could stand the heat. When they were wet with perspiration they headed for the nearest door. With a shout they rushed for a stream and plunged into the cold water! This was supposed to cure almost any disease. Men used the sweat house to make themselves clean before dancing or to remove body odor when going hunting. Others thought that heat made their legs stronger. Almost all agreed that the sweat house made them feel better and that it was one good way to keep clean.

Sweat houses were usually earth-covered except in the north where the roof was of planks covered with earth. In the northeast the sweat house had a dome-like shape covered with mats and earth. Unlike other California groups, the northeastern Indians "sweated" by means of steam made by pouring cold water on hot stones.

Sweat houses were made with greater care than other houses in the villages. Sometimes a very large sweat house was built, called a "dance house." Women were allowed to enter the dance houses when a special celebration was being held.

6   FROM ACORNS TO GRASSHOPPERS

Today, California's orchards and gardens produce food enough for the state, as well as for other states and even other countries. What did the Indians eat before there were cultivated plants? Except for the Yuman tribe, the California Indians never learned to plant and grow crops. Even though Indians fished in rivers, lakes, the ocean, and along the shores, and hunted wild game in the forests, most of their food came from plants that grew around them. A supply of food could be found with little work—acorns, seeds, nuts, fruits, roots, and leaves which could be cooked or eaten raw. If there was not enough of one kind of food, they looked for another. They moved from place to place as the various foods were ready to pick. In the spring there were plants such as clover and Indian's lettuce; in the summer there were fruits and berries; in the fall, acorns and seeds. The desert did not offer many foods but with careful searching some foods were found even there. A patient people, they never hurried or worried very much. What they couldn't find one day, they found another time in another place. Sometimes the Indians were short of certain foods but they did not starve.

The Indian was lucky to find so many oak trees in California, especially along the coast and on both sides of the big central valley. Women were the food-gatherers. In the fall when the oaks had ripe acorns, women left their homes in the village, usually as a group to make the harvest task happier. Each woman wore a woven, basket-like cap. A net which held a basket was slung across her forehead. In her hand she carried a smaller basket to be filled with acorns and then emptied into the larger net basket. The women laughed and sang as the baskets were filled to the brim with food for the months ahead. Women also wandered through the lowland plains and the foothill meadows when the grasses turned yellow. With seed-beaters they scooped tops of grasses or other seeds into shallow baskets. This time the net

Acorns were an important food. (Robert C. Frampton)

Seed-beaters and seed-gathering baskets. (Robert H. Lowie Museum of Anthropology, University of California, Berkeley)

baskets were filled with seeds for use during the winter months.

When the acorns had dried the children helped crack them with stones. The dry acorn seed covering had a brown, papery skin like that of a peanut. This skin had to be stripped off. Then the acorns could be pounded into meal with a stone mortar and pestle. Often the women went to a large rock in which there were small scooped-out holes where they pounded the acorns. We can imagine that they enjoyed pounding in time to their singing or chatting. When they were not singing, they could talk over the latest village news.

After the pounding, the bitter taste had to be removed from the acorn meal. To do this a little hill of sand was made and the center scooped out. Large leaves were put in the bottom and the meal was placed on top of them. Water was poured over the meal several times. It seeped through the meal and down through the sand. Now the meal was no longer bitter and was ready to be made into a mush. Sometimes water was poured over the meal in a basket. A lazier way was to bury the hulled acorns in a wet, swampy place for several months. Indians thought that this also took the bitter taste out of the acorns.

Now the sweetish, pink meal had to be cooked. There were no pots or pans, so meal and water were put into a tightly-woven basket. With a looped stick, hot stones were dropped into the water. Women had to stir the mush around and around as fast as they could so that holes would not be burned in the basket. Then the still bubbling hot mush was ready to be dipped into by eager fingers. The Indians liked this mush and probably thought about it the way we think about bread.

Water was heated and food was cooked in baskets with hot stones. (Arthur Barr Productions, Inc.)

Another food was the screwbean that came from mesquite bushes. (Robert C. Frampton)

Indians liked the chia seeds more than almost anything else. (Robert C. Frampton)

In desert areas, pottery bowls were used for cooking over fires. Some of the Indians were lucky enough to have strong soapstone jars and bowls. Cooking in these was much easier. Meat, seeds, roots, and other foods were cooked in baskets. Fish and meat were often roasted in a deep pit filled with red-hot coals or sometimes on a stick held over the fire.

All the California Indians used many kinds of seeds as food. Seeds were not pounded in a mortar but were usually ground on a hard stone slab called a *metate*. With another stone like a small rolling pin (*mano*), women ground seeds into meal. Seed meal was cooked in the same way as acorn meal.

Another food came from mesquite bushes. On the desert the mesquite bushes hung heavy with long, brown, pod-like beans. In a good year the ground was covered with the ripe pods. These were sweet and good to eat. Green pods could be picked from the trees in the summer and were dried and stored like acorns.

When they were needed, pods were pounded in a mortar. The meal was put in a pot or jar and soaked. Meal could be mixed with water and used as a drink. It could be made into a dough and baked in hot sand. Sometimes little hard balls of meal were carried for food on a journey. It could also be cooked, stored in a pit, and left for about a month. From time to time water was poured on it. When ready to be eaten it was brown and sweet like molasses.

The *chia,* a kind of sage, had seeds in early summer. Indians called it *pa-sal.* They liked these seeds more than almost anything else and could live on them for weeks. Dried *chia* seeds, rich in oil, were pounded into meal and cooked. Uncooked *chia* seeds were taken on trips and could be eaten this way also.

Cactus (*na-vit*) grew in the mountains and desert. The seeds of the cactus (*mu-tal*), the fruit, and even the stalks were eaten. A small cactus (*ma-nai*), ripe in summer, was full of sweetness. The flat joints were brushed to take off the sharp spines. Then they were dried, stored, and boiled when needed.

The seeds, fruit, and the stalks of the cactus were eaten. (Robert C. Frampton)

Yucca was an important source of food and fiber. (Robert C. Frampton)

Yucca was important as a food and for fiber. It could be found on hillsides, in sandy canyons, and on desert slopes. The fruit with big, black seeds was picked when green. Roasted in hot coals, it had a taste something like that of a green apple. When ripe, the fruit was sweet and juicy. The stem of the yucca was roasted in pits with hot coals and this was a real treat. Fibers of the yucca were used for nets, baskets, mats, sandals, straps, cradles, and even hairbrushes. When yucca roots were pounded, they produced a foam used as soap.

Piñon nuts or pine nuts, which we still eat today, were used by many tribes. The small pine cones were pulled or beaten from the trees with a forked stick. The tight little cones were then piled in a heap and roasted until they popped open. Then the piñon nuts were shaken out. Piñon nuts were just as good as candy to Indians and they could keep them to eat anytime.

The *agave* (century plant) was used mostly by desert tribes. In April, the agave formed stalks that looked like huge asparagus stems. Stones were heated in fire pits; agave stalks were placed in the pits and covered with grass and earth. There they roasted for a day or two until they were sweet and delicious—something like asparagus.

Wild plums, called *yslay* by the Indians, grew high up in the mountains. The plums were mostly seeds which were taken out and crushed in a mortar. After the meal was washed as acorn meal, it was eaten.

Indians were very fond of the good-tasting piñons that came from pine-tree cones. (Robert C. Frampton)

Agave was food for the desert tribes. (Rancho Santa Ana Botanic Garden, Claremont— M & M Carothers)

Palms grew in desert areas, near pools, or where water seeped into sandy places. Dates from them were as good to eat then as they are today.

The low, evergreen juniper trees had bluish, marble-sized berries. The Cahuilla of southern California liked them especially and called them *wut*. *Manzanita* gave berries for food and could be squeezed to make a sort of cider. The bright red berries of the lemonade berry made a drink the Indians liked. The red berries of the *toyon* which ripen at Christmas were not so sweet but they were eaten also. Purple elderberries were found in many places throughout the state.

From the great yellow water lily, the Klamath Indians took unripe seed pods. They were sun-dried and a meal made from them. This meal, called *woka,* could be stored for a long time.

Of all the tribes, only the Mohaves and the Yumas grew any plants. Others probably thought that there were enough plants growing wild. In later years the mission padres taught the Indians how to grow and harvest many crops.

Women gathered food plants but men brought in meat. Some deer were caught in brush-covered pits along deer trails. A deer hunter took a stuffed deer head and placed it on his own. In this way the deer was fooled into believing that the Indian was another deer. When he came close, the arrow whizzed from the bow and down went the deer!

Rabbit was the day-to-day meat and there always seemed to be plenty of it. Rabbits were not only good for food but their fur was useful. They were caught in pits as well as with bow and arrow. Another way was to throw a curved rabbit stick and hit the rabbit. Rabbit sticks could be thrown straight and hard and were also used to catch birds. Another way to catch rabbits was with nets. Whole families of Indians spread out in a line. Hunters beat at the shrubs and drove rabbits into the long, low nets. Rats, mice, and squirrels were trapped also. All of

When deer-hunting, the Indian tried to look and act like a deer. (Arthur Barr Productions, Inc.)

them were either roasted over a fire or made into a soup. Indians did not eat coyotes or grizzly bears. Both of these animals were respected, for the Indians thought the coyote was supposed to be an evil spirit, the bear a good spirit.

When food was scarce the Indians even ate grasshoppers, worms, giant ants, or caterpillars. These were usually roasted. Large roasted grasshoppers were a favorite food! We know that tribes in the south ate snakes and certain lizards.

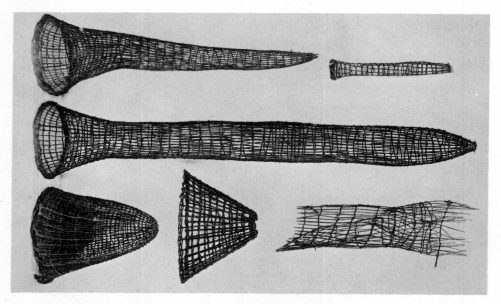

Fish traps. (Robert H. Lowie, Museum of Anthropology, University of California, Berkeley)

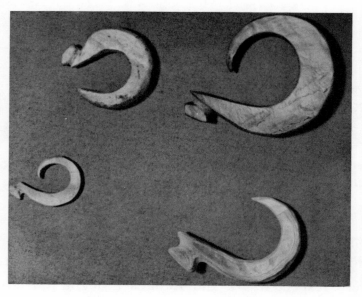

Fishhooks made from shells. (Southwest Museum, Los Angeles)

Plenty of fish were found in the rivers and ocean. Shellfish and mussels were taken from the sea or gathered along the shore. Sometimes whales came near enough to be pulled ashore. Then the fishermen of the village took to their boats with pointed harpoons. When they were lucky every family in the village had a feast! Besides fish there were many clams and crabs. Rivers were full of all kinds of fish, especially salmon in the northern streams. When salmon came up the rivers in the spring many were caught. This was a time for feasting and celebration.

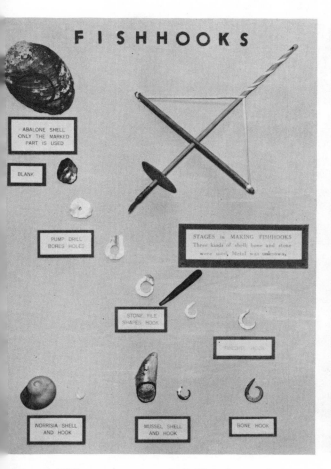

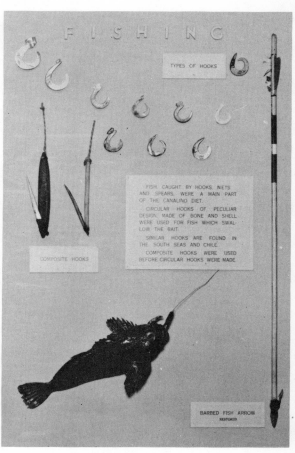

Different types of fishhooks and how they were made. (Exhibit, Santa Barbara Museum of Natural History—Bosworth Lemere, Photographer)

Nets were used more than fishhooks for catching fish. On the southern coast in deep waters, shell fishhooks were used, and sometimes a harpoon that looked like a spear. The long slender shaft was pushed forward, not thrown. A heavier harpoon that

The harpoon that looked like a spear was pushed forward, not thrown. (Exhibit, Los Angeles County Museum)

was thrown was used by the northwest tribes to catch sea lions.

Large nets and dip nets were known to all the Indians. They knew the best kind to use whether they were catching fish in streams or from the seashore. Nets had floats of wood or tule stems. Notched flat rocks made by Indians have been found. We believe that they were "sinkers" used to stretch and hold the nets in the water.

Indians liked to flavor their food with salt if they could get it. A salt plant grew in northern California near the redwood area. Here the Indians gathered the big leaves and stems of the salt plant. These were spread in the sun until wilted and then rolled up into balls. The balls were put on redwood slabs and slowly heated until they changed into ashes which were almost pure salt. In the Mendocino area there were salt springs around

A favorite drink was made from the berries of the manzanita. (Robert C. Frampton)

Indians liked to eat raw onions. (Robert C. Frampton)

which crusts of salt covered the ground and plants. Indians for miles around made journeys to get salt there and took enough to last them for at least a year.

We know something of what the Indians ate by the things we find buried. In places where villages once stood, huge black areas mark places where fires once burned. Bones of deer, sea lions (or seals), rabbits, and birds show some of the things they ate. Old shell heaps or mounds show us some of their food taken from the ocean. Old pestles, mortars, *metates, manos,* spoons, tools, and jars, or pieces of them, tell us how they must have prepared their food.

Here is a list of foods eaten by the Indians and the ways in which they cooked their food:

Ground in Mortars	*Sun-Dried*	*On Flat Rock*	*Drinks*
Acorns	Berries	Acorn cakes	Lemonade berries
Wild cherry seeds	Plums	Cherry pit cakes	Manzanita berries
Manzanita	Seaweeds		
Cattail stems	Fish		
Cactus seeds	Meat		
Sunflower seeds			

Eaten Raw	*Cooked over the Fire*	*Roasted*	*Boiled*
Fish	Deer	Yucca shoots	Acorn mush
Shellfish	Fish	Yucca stalks	Cherry seed mush
Pine nuts	Whale	Bulbs	Buckeye seeds
Wild onion	Duck	Fish	Cattail seeds
Toyon berries	Quail	Cattail stems	Chia seeds
Grapes		Birds	Grass seeds
Wild cherries		Meat	Mushrooms
		Grasshoppers	Cactus fruit
			Fish
			Meat
			Birds

7 THE INDIAN FAMILY AT HOME

THE mother of the family was the chief worker. From sunrise to sunset she had plenty to do; her tasks never seemed to be finished. She was up at daybreak to get water and a few sticks of wood for the fire. A light breakfast was eaten by the family and then each member went to his day's work.

Most of the day the mother spent pounding meal or gathering and preparing any other kinds of food. She took the girls with her when she went to the woods nearby to find ripe berries, juicy bulbs, or sweet-smelling herbs. Their bright eyes helped the mother to find plants they knew were good for food. When the mother did have time to sit down, her hands were not idle. Baskets and other useful things for the family had to be made. No one told her what to do; she knew all too well.

Men also arose soon after the sun came up. After breakfast they were ready to start their day's work. They did the heavy work of gathering wood for building and finding stones for mor-

The mush was dipped into with eager fingers. (Arthur Barr Productions, Inc.)

tars. Some days the father of the family went with net, spear, or bow and arrow to get meat or fish. The California hunter was not as daring a hunter as Indians elsewhere. Even though he liked meat, it sometimes seemed too much work to get it. When the father of the family had time to spend at home, there were many things to be made—everything from new houses and canoes to stone tools and ornaments. In the afternoon after going to the sweat house, he liked to sit in the sun with his village friends and have a game or talk over their plans for the village people.

In the evening the family had the main meal of the day. The father ate slowly as he talked to his family about what he had done that day. The mother and the children showed respect by being silent. After the meal he was ready to go to the sweat house for a good night's sleep.

When all was quiet in the little house, the mother or grand-mother, if there was one, sat with the children around the fire. This was a good story time. The mother had a sort of sing-song story she told. She liked to tell of the places she could remember that meant something to her—the mountains, the high trees, the dancing waterfalls. Grandmother's stories were more exciting for she had many animal tales. The bear, she told them, was the first one to live on earth. He was a powerful animal who should be respected. Children liked most to hear about the coyote, the clever animal that was always playing tricks. After the tiny light of the fire died down, there was nothing to do but go to sleep.

Indian children did some work but most of the time they were free to do as they pleased. A daughter would help to care for the smaller children in the family. It was not unusual for her to carry a baby brother or sister strapped in a cradle on her back. Girls learned to do most of the things around the house that the mothers did. They started making baskets when quite young, small ones at first. Both the mother and grandmother taught the girls how to pound in the mortar and cook their simple food.

Even though there were no schools there were many things that both boys and girls had to learn. Boys were taught by their fathers to make bows and small tools. They learned how to skin deer, rabbits, or other animals. Sometimes the boys climbed into the leafy trees and brought down tiny eggs from birds' nests. Fathers led their sons into the valleys and up the cliffs of the canyons when they went hunting and fishing. The father or grandfather taught them how to throw the curved stick to catch a rabbit.

Curved rabbit sticks.

A father knew exactly the land that belonged to the village and the territory of his tribe. He had been taught this by his father. It was said that each Indian knew his own territory "by the soles of his feet" for he had gone over it so many times. It was important that the sons of the family know all about the tribal territory, too. When boys grew older they were taught the songs, dances, and beliefs of the tribe. There were no books, of course, and so they had to have good memories.

Boys were given tests for bravery. They might be pushed into an ant's nest or be lashed with a willow switch. Those who cried or fought back would not be brave, the older men thought. Boys were made to run many miles so that their legs would be strong.

All Indian children were taught by their fathers and mothers how to behave. Some of the rules they learned were:

Be good to older people
Tell the truth
Do not get angry
Be polite to everyone
Speak softly
Be brave and do not be afraid

They were told that if they did these things they would "grow old in good health." The older men said, "You will be able to tell your own children about these things. Then you can go to the sky to live when old. If you do not, a rattlesnake or a spider may bite you. Whether this happens or not, you will always have bad luck if you do not do the things taught to you."

8 BOATS, BOWS, AND TOOLS

INDIAN men were always busy doing other things besides building houses, going hunting, and fishing. They were very clever with their hands. Much of their time was spent building boats and making tools. In the beginning these early-day people had no iron or other metal. There were no axes, saws, knives, hammers, or nails. Once again we find that the Indians had to make what they could with the materials they had.

All the coastal Indians and those along rivers or lakes had to have boats. Two materials were used: wood and tule. Boats had to be used on swift, tumbling rivers as well as on quiet lakes. Others were used near the seashore but the strongest and best ones were used on the open sea.

Indians in the northwest built very strong redwood canoes although they looked heavy and clumsy. This kind of canoe was dug out rather crudely from half a redwood log, and was square on the ends and round on the bottom. Seats for the paddlers were carved in the log. Long, heavy paddles were used both as

The Chumash made better boats than any other Indian tribe. (Santa Barbara Museum of Natural History)

paddles for rowing and for pushing the boat through the water. In the northeast, boats of pine, cedar, or fir were shaped by burning or chopping the logs with a sharp stone.

The wooden boat of the Chumash was the best one made in California or even in the United States. The Chumash painted their boats and often put designs of bright colors on them. This plank boat, or *tomolo,* as it was called, could be used in the rough waters of the ocean. It was used along the shore from Point Concepción to San Diego and across to the Santa Barbara Islands. Island Indians used them to visit the mainland. When a boatload of Indians came paddling to the mainland shore, village children ran shouting to meet them. Village people were excited as they gathered around to greet the visitors. Children had a happy time when their fathers took them fishing in the *tomolos.*

The Chumash boats were split planks that had been scraped and smoothed. Holes were drilled or burned along the edges of

Chumash Indians "sewed" the planks together (view of bottom of boat). (Southwest Museum, Los Angeles)

Tule boats were made from long bundles of tule tied together with plant-fiber string. (Arthur Barr Productions, Inc.)

each plank. Indians "sewed" the planks together with strong cords. Black, sticky tar or asphalt found along beaches was used to seal the seams and holes. The boats had double paddles. With them the men could shoot through the water. Explorers were surprised to see such wonderful boats and said that they "seemed to fly through the water." Such boats were twelve to twenty-two feet long and could carry from two to twelve people.

For traveling on the bays, a light tule boat was all that was needed. Even these boats could be paddled for some distance. Almost all the tribes used them. Bundles of tule were formed into flat boats, very long and high at each end. The tule boats were so light that they floated high on top of the water. Tule boats moved so quietly through the water that fish were not frightened away. The several men who went in them paddled with their feet while they were busy catching fish with nets or spears.

A bundle of tules tied together into a raft was enough to keep it afloat. The tule raft was "poled" rather than paddled.

Some of the tribes lived near small streams and did not need boats. If women and children wished to cross a stream, they crowded into very large baskets. Men waded into the water and pushed the baskets across the narrow river.

Boats were important to Indian life but so were bows and arrows, and the men made many of them. The best bows were made of wood from the elderwood, laurel, and bay trees. The very finest ones were of juniper wood. Wide strips of deer sinew were used for backing the bows, these being glued on with glue made from deer's horns and hoofs. When finished the bows were usually painted and decorated with designs.

Most arrow shafts were made from the heart of the button willow tree. When this wood could not be found, cane or bamboo was used. Indians were clever about making the slender shafts very straight. First they had to make a groove in a flat stone. The stone was heated until very hot. The arrow shaft was dipped into water and run through the groove of the hot stone. In this way the arrow shaft was steamed until very straight.

Arrow straighteners. (Robert H. Lowie, Museum of Anthropology, University of California, Berkeley)

After this, the arrow shaft was ready for the arrowhead or arrow point. Arrow points had to be of the hardest and finest stones that could be found. Indians liked the shiny, black, hard, volcanic glass called obsidian the best. The arrow point maker shaped the obsidian or other hard rock with a stone tool, chipping it into shape bit by bit. This was not easy and took great

Any size or kind of arrow point needed by the hunter could be slipped into the main shaft of the arrow. (Arthur Barr Productions, Inc.)

care and patience. The base of the point was so notched that it could be fastened to the arrow shaft. As he bound the point to the shaft with sinew, the Indian chewed the sinew to make it soft. When the sinew was dry, the point was fastened even more securely with asphalt. Feathers were split and bound to the

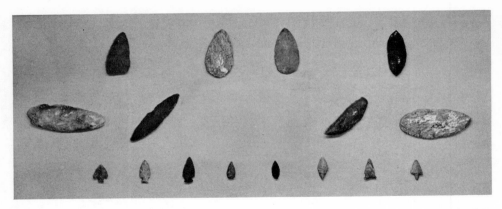

Arrow points and spear points. (Santa Barbara Museum of Natural History—Bosworth Lemere Photo)

other end of the shaft. When bound in a spiral, the arrow could sail a long distance through the air. The bowstrings were made of twisted sinew or very strong plant fiber. Arrows were carried in a skin bag with the hide side turned in to protect the arrows. Men of all tribes were good arrow makers. They knew that fine arrows and bows were needed for hunting or for fighting if that was necessary. The Yurok made such fine bows and arrows that other tribes were glad to either buy or trade to get them. Larger points were made for spears but they were not used very much.

Narrow, thin pieces of stone were used for borers to make holes in various objects such as beads. Crude hammers and axes were made from hard stones. A tough, solid rock was best for mortars, pestles, drills, and tools. Obsidian and hard flint stone were flaked into knives or blades used for skinning animals. Sharp-edged

All they had to shape the steatite bowls were crude, pointed stones. (Southwest Museum, Los Angeles)

razor clam shells were also made into knives. Wedges or chisels were made from deer's horns and among the Chumash, whale bones were used. Pipes for smoking were shaped from soapstone (steatite) or from certain other soft stones and woods. Needles and flutes were made from bones. Spoons and cooking paddles were of wood or deer's horns. Curved, wooden rabbit sticks had

Yurok acorn gruel spoons made from elk antlers.

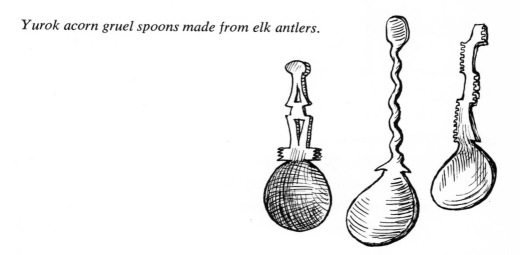

to be carefully shaped. Many hours of work were necessary to make all these things.

Nets of all sizes were used for fishing in fresh waters and still bays. The material for them was made from bark fibers or the outside fibers of Indian hemp and milkweed. The pulp was pounded to remove the fiber. Then the Indian would twist and

It took many hours of work to shape rock into bowls. (Santa Barbara Museum of Natural History)

roll the fibers up and down along his legs until a strong string was made. In the Shastan tribe area and in the northwest, iris grew and from them came thin, tough fibers for nets. The fibers were hard to get but the string made from them was thin and tough. Agave fibers made a course, stiff string. Sometimes the sharp spine at the tip of the agave leaf was left on a string of agave fiber to make a perfect needle and thread! Grapevine was used for tying large articles.

Charmstones, pendants, and ornaments of many kinds were shaped from smooth, well-polished stone. Not the least important things that the men made were fishhooks from shells of various kinds. Men were also the fire makers. Fire was made by striking two pieces of hard stone together, or by a drill twirled by hand, until a spark flew out and was caught in a small pile of tinder or dried sticks and grass.

Although Indian men are sometimes thought of as being lazy, they had to spend many hours hunting, gathering materials, and making boats, tools, weapons, and other necessities of everyday life.

The sharp spine and fiber of the agave made a good needle and thread. (Robert C. Frampton)

9 CLEVER HANDS
AND NIMBLE FEET

Baskets and Basket Making

INDIAN women spent many hours of their days weaving baskets. They must have enjoyed the art of basket making, for the weaving of materials, colors, and designs show their skill. They made many kinds because baskets were important in their way of life. Baskets were of various sizes, from small treasure baskets to large food storage ones. With few materials and many hours of patient work baskets of great beauty were made.

Baskets were either twined or woven. Most Indians used only one of these methods, but some of the central California women (Yuki, Maidu, Yokuts) used both. Twined baskets were well known to all Californians but the northern tribes made them especially well.

Twining is much like weaving. As the women wove the soft materials in and out between stiff rods or ribs (like an um-

Soft materials were twined in and out between the stiff rods. (Arthur Barr Productions, Inc.)

brella), they pulled the ribs upward to form the sides of the basket. The ribs were usually small hazel or willow roots, and they used strips of root from pine, redwood, or spruce trees for the twining material. They twined the strips tightly around each rib so that the basket would be tight and firm. Some of these

The Mono women wove feathers along the rims of their baskets. (Santa Barbara Museum of Natural History—Bosworth Lemere Photo)

twined baskets were loosely woven for carrying baskets, seed-beaters, traps, baby cradles, or for draining water through meal.

Coiling is more like sewing or stitching. Basket weavers who coiled made a start with one or more long thin reeds or a small bundle of long straws. Each row was sewed to the one before, row after row, around and around until the basket was the right size and shape. There were no needles, of course, so sharp bone awls were used to make a hole for each stitch. The basket was finished by stitching twice around the top coil. Then the extra stitching material was cut off with a stone knife. You can imagine how proud the Indian woman was when her beautiful basket was completed!

Baskets were usually shaped like rounded bowls, some large and some small. In the south, baskets were made with a shoulder and with a small neck. A few tribes wove baskets with no shoulders which were called "bottle neck" baskets. The women's caps were tightly woven and were made round to fit the head. The

Pomo burden basket design.

caps of the southern California Indians were cone-shaped. Mats were loosely woven or twined like the baskets. Baby-carrying cradles were of many styles, mostly of the lying-down kind. The Pomo wove a sitting-up type of cradle.

The Pomo women were the finest basket makers in the United States. Their baskets were works of art. The Santa Barbara Chumash made fine ones also. Both the fine weaving and the

Bits of shell decorated the baby carrying-cradle.

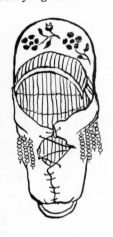

Types of cradles. (Robert H. Lowie Museum of Anthropology, University of California, Berkeley)

The Pomo women made baskets of great beauty. (Santa Barbara Museum of Natural History—Bosworth Lemere Photo)

designs were extremely well done. The Pomo baskets were different from others. Pomo women wove bright, soft feathers in and out all over the basket. The smallest baskets looked like a downy hummingbird's nest! They even wove lids for their baskets, which very few other tribes did. There were tribes that wove a few feathers along the rim of baskets or strung shells that dripped along the sides. All these fine baskets were famous and were worth a good deal in trading.

Tiny feathers were woven into the Pomo gift baskets. (Santa Barbara Museum of Natural History—Bosworth Lemere Photo)

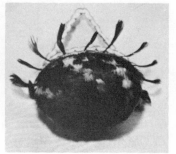

Baskets were important to them and they wove many kinds. (Robert H. Lowie Museum of Anthropology, University of California, Berkeley)

Some baskets had woven lids.
(Santa Barbara Museum of Natural
History—Bosworth Lemere Photo)

The Colorado Indians made the poorest baskets. For the most part, theirs were loosely-woven traps for wild animals or fish. The best baskets they had came to them in trade from neighboring tribes.

One can well imagine the many hours it took to find all the materials needed for basket making. Women wandered through the woods near the village looking for grasses, roots, and stems

The bark of the redbud was peeled off and used for the red designs. (Rancho Santa Ana Botanic Garden, Claremont—M & M Carothers Photo)

Women took great care in finding the right grasses, roots, and stems for their baskets. (Arthur Barr Productions, Inc.)

useful for basket designs. Dyes for the colored designs came from plants also. All but the black were made with grass or reeds. Designs made with grass were light brown at first and became darker as they aged. Reeds were soaked in mud or dyed in berry juice to make the colors wanted. Redbud, which gave the red color, was the plant most used. White, black, and some red dyes were made from the alderwood tree. Black stems of certain ferns made fine black designs. "Overlay" designs were made by twining the design on the outside of the basket. Coiled baskets had designs both inside and outside.

Weaving and design was taught to girls by their mothers. For this reason, the baskets and designs of each family group were about the same through the years. The designs had meanings

Yokuts basket designs

Flies

Flies

Deer foot

Water snake markings

Deer foot

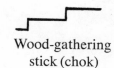

Wood-gathering
stick (chok)

Arrow points

Tied in the middle

Crooked

Arrow point

Crooked

Crooked

Rattlesnake markings

Millipede

Rattlesnake markings

King snake markings

King snake markings

Rattlesnake markings

77

Rattlesnake design basket.
(Southwest Museum,
Los Angeles)

and told stories known only to the women of each tribe. The designs ran in straight or broken bands around the baskets. Some had triangles, stars, birds, animals, or flowers. A design that ran around the basket like a snake (called the rattlesnake design) was used in rattlesnake ceremonies. It was believed that the basket maker who completely closed her design would become blind, so women left a break in their designs instead of joining them together and this break was called a *dau*.

The designs in the baskets did not always join. (Southwest Museum, Los Angeles)

Cahuilla painted storage jar.

Pottery

Basket making is an older art than pottery and few California Indians except those in desert areas made any pottery. Even this pottery was not too well-made. The Yuma, Mohave, and Colorado River tribes made pottery that was good enough for their daily needs: cooking and food bowls and pots, water and storage jars.

When making jars, crushed rock was mixed with clay and this mixture became dullish-red when baked. The wet clay was first rolled into long, sausage-shaped pieces. A flat pancake of clay was made as a base for each jar or pot. Then the rolls of wet clay were coiled on top of the base, one roll on top of the other, around and around until the jar was formed. It was patted and shaped with the fingers and with a small smooth stone. The pots were then ready to be dried in the sun. Most of the pots had very simple designs painted on them. The last step was to bake the jars in a bed of hot coals to make them hard and strong.

Mohave bowl and ladle with "rain" and "fish backbone" designs.

Mohave pottery bowl with "cottonwood leaf and rain" design.

Dancing

Indians had many kinds of dances. There was a dance when a baby was born and a mourning dance when anyone in the village died. There were hunting dances, thanksgiving dances, dances when boys and girls became young men and women. There were wedding dances and many dances that had to do with religion.

When spring came, bringing the cheery songs of birds, green hills, and many-colored flowers, it was a perfect time for dancing. When the juicy new clover was ready for picking and eating, Indians danced for joy. In northern California, Indians were glad when they heard a shout through the village of *"Nepeg-wuh"* ("the salmon"), for that meant that the first salmon of the season had been seen. That night there was sure to be a "salmon dance."

In the fall, when the acorns and seeds were ripe, Indians had a thanksgiving dance. They also celebrated the beginning of the hunting season. Seated around the fire, old men of the tribe told of the fat elk and deer that had been caught and dried for the winter months. Besides the meat, everyone knew that the animal skins would give them warm capes and blankets. Women told of the many baskets of acorns and seeds they had gathered and stored. Each told of the things he had done or made. After the stories and feasting, the dancing began.

At some time during the year, usually the latter part of summer, there was a dance for the dead. A large pile of wood and food to be burned was made in a certain place in the village. In the evening around the fire there was wailing for all those who had died during the year. New clothing and baskets were brought as gifts to the dead. As the Indians danced, one gift after another was thrown into the flames. They danced faster and faster, wailed louder and louder until all the gifts had been burned. After that, names of the dead were never again spoken.

A favorite Indian dance was the Ghost Dance. The men painted themselves white and acted in a funny way, much as our clowns do. They pretended to be like the tricky coyote and as they danced they shouted, "Woo! Woo!" to frighten the people.

Music

No matter how simply the Indians lived, each tribe had some kind of music. Probably the strange, weird sounds were more like noise than music. Music to them was not a tune but more a humming, grunting, or chanting in time to the stamping of feet or the clapping of hands.

Men made flutes of bone or wood, some large and some quite

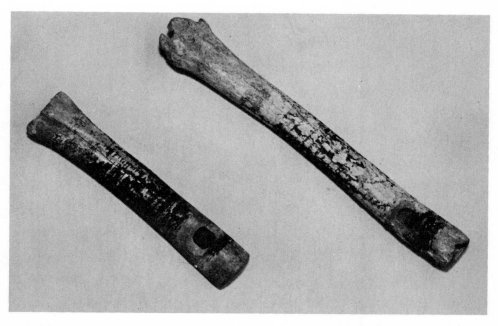

Men made flutes that would play a few notes. (Santa Barbara Museum of Natural History—Bosworth Lemere Photo)

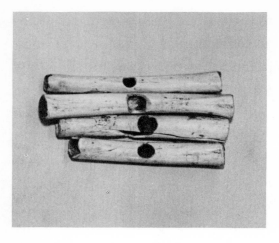

Some of the flutes were quite small. (Santa Barbara Museum of Natural History—Bosworth Lemere Photo)

small. Only a few notes could be played on any of them. The musician played by blowing across the holes of his flute. If a man could "sniff" or blow air from his nose across the holes, he was thought to be a good player. A wooden whistle used at ceremonies was so shrill that it could be heard above the chanting of the people.

Dancers used shell rattles. (Santa Barbara Museum of Natural History— Bosworth Lemere Photo)

Several kinds of rattles were used for dancing ceremonies. One rattle was made of two turtle shells put together with cherry seeds or small rocks inside. Another kind was made by tying deer hoofs on strings to a stick. Sometimes a man tapped on his bowstring and this made a sort of "twang." Medicine men had rattles made from dried cocoons filled with stones. A clacker was a split stick which made a rhythmic sound when beaten against the hand. A "bull roarer" was a wooden slab on a string that made a whirring sound when swung around in the air. The Luiseño tribe used the "bull roarer" to call each other or to announce the arrival of visitors. Drums were unknown in the earlier

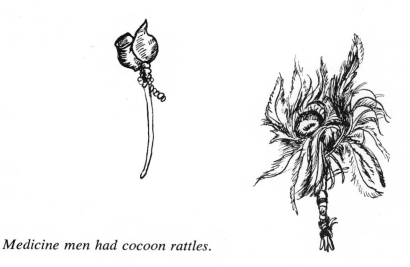

Medicine men had cocoon rattles.

years except as an Indian thumped on a log with his hands or a heavy stick.

You can imagine Indians outdoors on summer evenings, as they danced, sang, and told the old stories they had heard over and over again.

Pictographs and Petroglyphs*

Pictures that are painted on rocks are pictographs and those carved on rocks are petroglyphs. Hundreds of Indian petroglyphs still remain but there are only about seventy sites where pictographs have been found. Years have been spent in searching for these pictographs in mountain canyons and caves. Most of them have been found in the Shoshonean and Chumash areas. The ones found in caves have been better protected but even so, many of them are fading away. During the past years people did not know their value and many were destroyed. Pictures of the pictographs have been made with great care so that a record of them will not be lost.

The pictographs are painted in shades of red and brown and black and white. It is believed that the red and brown colors were made from colored rocks or ores (such as iron oxide) that were ground into powder and mixed with animal fat for an oil base. There are many places in the Chumash area where limestone is found and probably the white came from this kind of rock. Perhaps the black came from charcoal left in old fire holes. The red colors seem to have soaked into the rocks and so the red designs have lasted better than the others.

The crude designs are of men, animals, insects, the sun and stars, zigzags, triangles, circles, and the like. Perhaps the designs were painted on the rocks with fingers, a pointed stick, or with some plant fiber that was frayed and brush-like on the end. The petrographs were probably chipped into rocks with sharp stone tools.

What do these designs mean? How old are they? No one really knows. The answers to these questions went with the Indians who made them. It is believed that they were made by medicine men who wished to tell others of their thoughts. To us they appear to be a kind of Indian art but to the Indians they may have had some special meaning.

* Endsheets are sample of Pictograph.

84

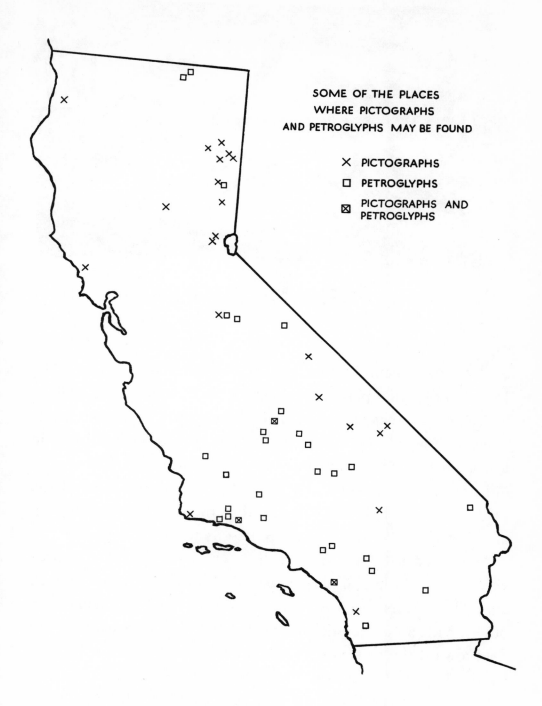

SOME OF THE PLACES
WHERE PICTOGRAPHS
AND PETROGLYPHS MAY BE FOUND

✕ PICTOGRAPHS

☐ PETROGLYPHS

⊠ PICTOGRAPHS AND
    PETROGLYPHS

10   INDIANS AT PLAY

No one, whether young or old, can work all the time. The Indians knew that play was important, too. Almost every village had a space either large or small where games of various kinds could be played. Sometimes one village played against those in a neighboring village and this was good fun for all. Those who did not play, both old and young, stood along the sides of the field to watch. You can imagine that the watchers jumped up and down and became just as excited as we do at a game!

Men liked to play a game called "shinny." The playing area was set up a little like our football field with goal posts at each end. The players, from two to fifteen men, lined up facing each other. With a curved stick a wooden ball was driven down the field toward the goal post. The team whose ball got to the post by the fewest strokes was the winner. If there were only two players they raced down the field side by side. This fast game was fun for both watchers and players. Lucky was the player whose head was not batted instead of the ball!

The hoop and pole game was played the most, except in the northwest area. It was played with a small hoop or a circle of willow branch wound with a fiber string, and with a long pole. The pole when thrown was supposed to fall through the rolling hoop. Each time it did a point was made and so many points made a game.

The Miwok women played a game something like our basketball. A deerskin ball was stuffed with grass or something else soft. Each player had two baskets shaped like seed-beaters, one

Everyone seemed to like the hoop and pole game. (Arthur Barr Productions, Inc.)

a little larger than the other. Players stood in a line. When the ball was thrown into the air, each player tried to catch it in the large basket. Whoever did, put the smaller basket over the ball so that it would not roll out. Then she raced with it down the field to the goal.

Men and women did not usually play games together but once in a while they had a "tug of war." Men and boys were on one side and women and girls on the other. Each side tried to pull the other one over a center line. It was a great joke when men let go of their end. Then the women and girls went laughing and tumbling to the ground!

These were field games but Indians liked sitting-down games also. Guessing games were played by men, dice games by women. One sitting-down game was something like our game of "Button, Button, Who Has the Button?" This game was sure to be played whenever Indians met together in a group. Not all tribes played the game alike but the idea was about the same. In this game there were two or more players on each side. An older man sat near the players to settle quarrels and see to it that they did not cheat. Each side had singers and as the game went on, they swayed and sang loudly. They must have been much like our cheerleaders at a game! The singers were supposed to bring good luck to their side.

Two sticks or bones small enough to be held in a man's hand were used. One was plain and one marked by a string around it or painted with a band in the center. The holders of the bones or sticks hid their hands under a skin or blanket. The pieces were passed one to the other. The side that was guessing pointed quickly to the hand it thought had the marked stick or bone. If right, it was the other side's turn to do the hiding. If not, the first side hid the piece again. Sometimes black and white pieces were used and players had to guess who had the white one. Ten or twelve sticks were stuck into the ground. Each time a side guessed right, it was given one of the sticks. The game was won when one side or the other won all the counting sticks. Games like this lasted for hours, sometimes all night, and there was much betting as to which side would be the winner. The Mohaves had a different way of playing. One player stuck a small stick into one of four little sand hills. In which hill was the stick hidden? That was the game.

Women liked dice games (Chemehuevi filled shells).

Among Indian women dice games took the place of today's card games. Women dressed in their nicest skirts and fancy woven basket caps. On went their very best necklaces, bracelets, and earrings. Then they were ready to go to a "dice party." The dice were round pieces of shell, sticks, tiny rocks, or nut shells that had been filled with tar. Whatever was used, a number of dots or designs were painted on one side of the dice. If the side that had the dots on it came up, so many points were counted. If the other side came up there were no points.

Many tribes played a ring and pin game. Rings were put on a string and fastened to a pointed stick. The game was to toss up the rings and catch them on the stick. Rings were made of many things such as acorns with the center pushed out to make a hole, or shells with holes in the center.

Nearly all games played by grown people were gambling games. They would bet with everything from shell money and deerskins to baskets and beads. They would even lose their food or houses if they bet and did not win.

Indian children loved to play. There were no schools, of course, and so life was like a long vacation for them until they began to grow up.

Girls had dolls that would seem strange to our girls today. Some of the dolls were only a deerskin wrapped around a stick. Some were of grass and others were made of clay. Nearly all the little girls had tiny doll cradles made like those for the baby of the family.

Boys were given small bows and arrows. They did not really use them but only pretended that they were hunting. They liked tops made with acorns that had little sticks in them. Boys tried to see whose top would spin the longest.

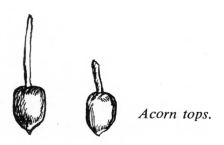

Acorn tops.

Small children played a game something like our hopscotch. They tried to see how far they could hop on one leg. The Miwok children played a game of hide-and-go-seek and also tag. The Pomo children played a game with a fiber ball in a ring. When a player batted the ball out of the ring he was "out." The last player to be "out" was the winner. Children were lucky who lived near the ocean, lakes, or a river, for they could go swimming.

It is surprising to find that Indians in that faraway time liked to play and that many of their games were much like the ones we have today.

11 SOMETHING OF VALUE:
TRADING AND SHELL MONEY

THE Indians had no money as we know it today, but they had to have something that could be used for trading with one another. Their money was made from things around them that had the most value. They used shells for money, not just any shells but special ones. The common shell was the clamshell and so their cheapest money (as we would think of pennies and nickels) were made of clamshell disks. These disks were rather round and about the size of a nickel (called *so*). Clamshells were broken into pieces, then rounded and polished on a sandstone slab. The thicker the clamshell disks the better the Indians liked them.

The disks were strung like beads. A long string was worth more than a short one. The clamshell money that was the oldest or that had the best polish, had the most value. Money was measured by wrapping the string around the palm of the hand, the fingers, or the closed fist, once or twice or several times. A short string was measured just once around the hand and was worth very little. Some tribes stretched the string of clamshell money out straight and measured it that way.

Clamshell shell money.

The small, thin, white, tooth-like dentalium shells were hard to find and so worth much more than clamshell money. These shells were found along the northern coast for the most part but they were used in other parts of the state. Strings of dentalium were usually about twenty-seven and a half inches long. The string was measured much as we would measure cloth without a yard-stick, by holding the string of shells from the thumb to the shoulder. The longer the string the more its worth, of course. If a man had several strings of dentalium money, he was thought to be very rich.

When white men first came to California they put certain values on strings of dentalium shells. A string of shells having eleven large dentalium was worth about fifty dollars. If there were twelve smaller shells, the string was worth twenty dollars; if thirteen, it was ten dollars. This was real "Indian money" and as such was used in trade for many other things.

The small, olive-shaped olivella shells were used nearly every-where in the state. In the north they were strung whole; in central and southern California, they were often broken up and rolled into thin disks. Neither kind had much value.

The haliotis shell, which is a form of abalone, was broken into pieces and used in ornaments and necklaces and by those who lived away from the ocean who had no other kinds of shells. However, they were not used as money in most cases.

Strung dentalium shells were measured from the thumb to the shoulder. (Southwest Museum, Los Angeles)

The Pomo tribe took the hinges and curves of large clamshells and polished them into long pieces. These were valuable ornaments but were not used except for trading. Some tribes found a kind of soft rock that we call magnesite. They rubbed or ground this into tubes about one to three inches long. They then baked the tubes until the heat turned them pink, red, or brown. As the magnesite tubes were worn they became shiny. These were worth more than shell money, just as gold is worth more to us than silver.

There were other uses for shells. Indians used all the beautiful shells they found for pendants, hairpins, necklaces, bracelets, and earrings. These were valuable in trade to inland tribes where there were no shells.

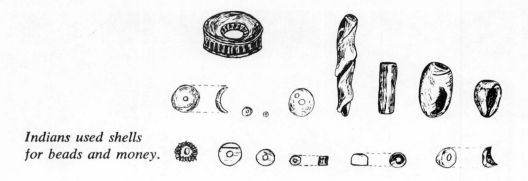

Indians used shells for beads and money.

A treasure worth almost as much as shell money was dried woodpecker scalps with soft red or green feathers. These were rare and since they were hard to get, they were valuable. The woodpecker scalps were traded for shell money or for any other wanted articles. Nothing was finer to wear to a dance or ceremony than a headband of red or green woodpecker scalps.

Deerskins that were either very light or very dark in color had great value. The common gray, light brown, or reddish-brown skins were not worth much in trade. The Yurok tribe thought that white deerskin was worth so much that it had to be kept in the family forever. To sell one of these was like a king selling his own crown!

Obsidian, the black volcanic glass, was worth about as much as dentalium or magnesite tubes. Red obsidian was very rare and was worth much more than the black. The longer the piece of obsidian, the more it was worth. Obsidian was used in some arrow points but it was more like a jewel to be worn and treasured. Large obsidian pieces were taken to dances and ceremonies and shown to visiting tribes. This proved that the owner was rich. Flint, a very hard stone, could be chipped very thin. It was worth a good deal also, especially if one had a long piece of it.

Men of the Wintun and Mohave tribes liked to travel and were good traders. They carried goods from tribe to tribe and their visits were usually welcomed. Other California Indians

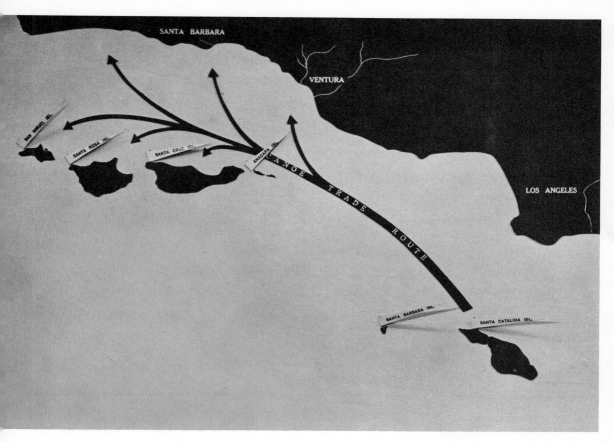

The trade route between island and mainland Indians. (Santa Barbara Museum of Natural History—Bosworth Lemere Photo)

did not roam about much but each group kept in its own territory most of the time. However, they did trade back and forth with their nearest neighbors. Indians along the coast traded fish and shells to forest Indians for acorns and animal skins. The Pomo traded their beautifully made baskets for the things they wanted from other tribes nearby. The Hupa Indians in the mountains traded with their neighbors, the Yuroks, who lived along the seashore. The Hupas gave seeds, nuts, and deerskins in return for redwood canoes, dried fish, and a salty seaweed they liked to eat. Indians near volcanic Mount Lassen made obsidian tools and arrow points from volcanic glass and traded them to valley Indians for blankets and acorns.

One of the most useful materials that all tribes wanted and few had was the steatite or soapstone found chiefly on Santa Catalina Island. Small picks and sharp stones were used to shape steatite into fine cooking bowls and other things such as charmstones. Steatite was mined and brought to the mainland in canoes and traded for sandstone bowls, beads, and food, especially acorns. It is believed that the large steatite bowls were made on the island. Smaller articles were made on the mainland, many of them from pieces of cooking pots. Even the pieces of steatite were worth a good deal in trade.

So we see that Indians did not always use shell money to buy what they wanted. They traded by giving something they had for things from other tribes. Everything had its own value, just as it does today.

Steatite was shaped into bowls, pendants, pipes, charmstones, and many other articles. (Exhibit, Santa Barbara Museum of Natural History—Bosworth Lemere Photo)

12 CHIEFS AND MEDICINE MEN: THEIR POWER AND MAGIC

INDIANS were usually an easygoing, free, and happy people. They had their own customs and rules and governed themselves quietly. No written laws were needed, no policemen or jails as we know them. People knew what they had to do. They knew that the chief of the village and the men of the council chosen by the people would see to it that their unwritten laws were obeyed. If people did not obey the rules, the chief and the council decided what had to be done. They were sometimes given a fine but most of the time the chief talked to them and told them that they had to get along with others and obey rules. This kind of government, by the chief, the council, and the people, kept peace in the village. One crime, however, was to take food given to the chief or headman that was supposed to be used by him when there were village feasts. If anyone dared to do this he might be killed. Rarely was there any fighting between villages or tribes unless food was taken without asking for it. A village or person that had a good supply had to protect it. Sometimes there were quarrels over acorn tree areas or fishing waters. Such quarrels were settled by the chiefs or headmen of the tribes. If there was fighting and anyone was killed, money was paid to the family of the person killed. The Yuma and Mohave were more warlike than other tribes and their chiefs were supposed to be very strong and brave.

Each band or village had a headman or chief. Usually he was made a chief because his father before him had been one. If he had no son, a brother or even his wife could be made the new chief. Sometimes the son was not a good man for a chief and then the people had to choose a chief. When the chief was chosen, it was because he had proven to be an important man in the village. Perhaps he had more shell money than the others or perhaps a rare white deerskin. He was supposed to know more than the rest of the people. He settled quarrels much like a judge but he did not rule the people. One of his duties was to plan when and where ceremonies were to be held. It was he who invited visitors to join in celebrations. He gave food to the poorer villagers. Everyone in a village believed that he belonged to a big family and that his neighbors in the village should be helped in time of need. Those who had plenty shared food and gifts with the chief. People said, "He gives to all who need it. Let us help him because he works for all of us." When the chief had no more to give the village people gave him more. When he said, "Let us sing" or "Let us dance," the people gathered together and had a happy time. Villagers believed that their chiefs could do no wrong. The Chumash and the Juaneño were known to have fought against any group not friendly to their chiefs.

More powerful than the chief was the village medicine man or *shaman*. His wrinkled brown face and body was usually painted with white, black, and red designs. Around his neck he wore

The medicine man or shaman sucked out pain with sucking tubes. (Los Angeles County Museum)

strings of animal teeth or animal claws. Small arrows were stuck into his matted hair. The Indians believed almost anything he told them. The "rain doctor" said that he could make rain whenever it was needed. The "snake doctor" could handle rattlesnakes and cure snake bites, so he said. The "bear doctor" said that he had the power to turn himself into a grizzly bear. When changed into a bear, he could kill all his enemies. Most of the Indians did not know whether or not to believe him. They were not sure what he could do, so they feared him.

The Indian medicine man's powers began when he was young. At the time of drinking the Jimsonweed (see chapter 13), he may have had dreams of becoming a medicine man. When he thought that he was ready to become one, he invited the villagers to a special ceremony. He told them of his great power to cure diseases. He told them that pains and diseases were caused by objects that had to be "sucked out" or "blown out" of their bodies or removed by some other magic means. So the medicine man sucked or blew, spurted water, rubbed or waved feathers. Suddenly a live spider or a very sharp stone appeared in his hand. These were the things that had caused the pain, he said. How he did this trick was his secret.

It was believed that charmstones brought good luck. (Santa Barbara Museum of Natural History—Bosworth Lemere Photo)

The medicine man or *shaman* thought that he gained power by going without food for a long time or by taking drugs that caused dreams. Dreams of animals in the "other world" were supposed to tell him what to do. People thought that he could talk to both the "good spirits" and the "bad spirits." They showed respect to him because they did not want him to talk to the "bad spirits" about them. One thing that almost all medicine men did know was the use of plants that cured diseases. When the medicine man cured the villagers everyone was happy. If he did not, he might be shot to death with arrows. Unlike other American Indian tribes the California Indians had medicine women as well as men. Medicine women were thought to have great power as doctors.

Some of the Chumash had another way of curing the sick or getting what they wanted. They placed twelve thin smooth stones in a circle and put some *chia* seeds in the middle. Over the *chia* they placed goose feathers and red dust. Three old men sat around the circle of stones and made strange noises. This kind of ceremony was supposed to cure the sick, bring rain, put out fires, bring fish, or help the tribe in case of war.

Charmstones of various shapes have been found that may have been "luck stones." Charmstones held over a stream would bring fish to the nets. Wild game would come toward the hunter if a charmstone were put on a rocky cliff. Arrows would not harm a warrior if he wore a charmstone about his neck.

A number of tribes, especially the Penutian family, had a secret society called *kuksu* or "big head dance." After painting their faces white to look like "spirits," men met in a large earth-covered house. The head of the society was a very important man. He was not only the chief of the village but was also a medicine man and the war chief of the village. He found places for acorn-gathering, made rain when needed, lit fires for ceremonies, and understood smoke signals. He made arrow poison if it was needed. In all ways he took care of the people of his tribe. When he called men to a meeting, he dressed in a very large, round, feather headdress and sometimes a feather cape. While the men beat drums, he sang and danced and told the people about how the world was made and how the Indians came to be. His songs were like prayers as he told of the things he wished for his people—good health, good crops, and freedom from all harm. When the head of the *kuksu* society did the "big head dance," the older members and the new ones knew that he would tell them many things they needed to know about their tribe. It made them happy to hear that there was someone who made the world and who took care of them.

Shaman's feather headdress.

13 OLD INDIAN BELIEFS
AND CUSTOMS

No one taught Indians about religion—where they came from or where they were going. Even though it was a mystery, Indians had their own ideas about such things. In the first place the Indians had great respect for everything they found in nature. To them the sun and the great redwood trees were very important. Some believed that in the beginning there was a Sky father and an Earth mother. From these two came all things. There were tribes that believed that the world was once a great mass. Out of the mass a god made the world and put it on the shoulders of seven giants. When one of the giants moved there was an earthquake. After the world, the god made animals and last of all he made man. Still others thought that animals made the world in the beginning. The Eagle was the maker and "good chief" of all. The Coyote with his sly ways was the "evil one."

Indians had great respect for the giant redwood trees. (United States Forest Service)

Indians believed that the mountains and streams had "spirits" in them. (California Division of Forestry)

The mountains and the streams had "spirits" in them, both good and bad, so they thought. Indians remembered these things when they wandered in the mountains or by rivers.

While there were those who thought there was one God, some believed in many gods. The one great god, so some believed, was *Chinigchinich*. If those in a village believed in him, an altar was built inside a round, mat-like fence. Eagle feathers and gifts of meal, tobacco, and arrows were offered to him on the altar. Sand paintings were carefully made by the altar as an offering also.

Sand paintings were made by the chief. (Southwest Museum, Los Angeles)

Indians did believe that there would be another life. The "other life" would be like this one except that there would be no trouble there. Everything they did in the "other life" would go well. The "Indian heaven" would be a place where there was plenty of time to sleep, to dance, and to have all the food they wanted to eat. Since the person would need things in the other world, some of his clothing, food, and treasures were buried (or burned) with him when he died.

Exhibit of Ceremonial Dress worn by the Pomo and Mohave tribes. (Santa Barbara Museum of Natural History—Bosworth Lemere Photo)

Indians did not pray for what they wanted; they danced and sang about their needs. They danced when they wanted luck in hunting, or to find something that would make them rich, or to be cured of an illness. When there was a new month, old men danced and sang, "As the moon dies and comes to life again, so we who die will live again." Chiefs, they believed, became stars in the sky and so they gave names to the stars.

Indians had many ceremonies even though they led simple lives. The age-old stories about the beliefs, customs, and ceremonies of Indian days have been passed down through the years. It is interesting to learn about some of these ceremonies that meant so much to the people of that long-ago time.

The Young Child

Soon after a child was born, it was tied to its cradle board. In this way the mother or an older child in the family could carry the baby about on her back. In cold weather a rabbit skin was thrown over the cradle to keep the baby warm. As the child grew older he ran about on sunny days with his mother. On foggy or cold days he stayed inside the house close to the fire. When he became six years old he was given a name. This was a time of celebration and village people met together for a "name-giving ceremony." The chief or headman held the child in his arms as he danced in a circle. As he did this, he gave the child the name. From that time on he was no longer thought of as a very young child.

Girls' Growing Up Ceremony

When a girl reached the age of thirteen or fourteen, she was thought to be a grown-up person. Girls often married at the age of fifteen. When girls became that age, they were made to lie on a bed of hot sand for three or more days. This was supposed to make them strong and good mothers some day. During this time, women danced around the girls, singing the old songs of the tribe. After this, the chief told the girls of the old beliefs of the tribe. He made a sand painting of the world on the ground. Looking at the sand picture, the girls thought about how the world was made. The chief told them that they were now old enough to be a part of the world. He made a lump of *chia* or sage seeds and salt and put it into the mouth of each girl. Each girl tasted the lump and dropped it into the sand picture. This was the way she made herself a part of the world. The picture was then swept away but the sage lumps were given back to the girls to keep among their treasures.

The Luiseño added to this custom by having the girls run a race to a rock near the village. Here the chief's wife painted designs on the girls' faces and put the same designs on the rock. Once a month, for four months, the girls were brought back to the rock. Each time a different design was used. After that they were thought to be true members of the Luiseño tribe.

A girl was tattooed on her chin just before she was married. All the Indians of the Pacific coast did this. They thought that the tattoos made girls more beautiful. It may not have made the girls beautiful but everyone could tell by the tattoos that they were married.

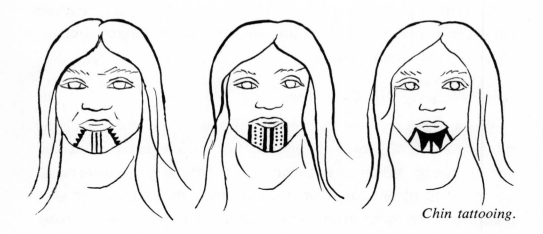

Chin tattooing.

Boys' Growing Up Ceremony

Boys had to go through even more than girls when they became fourteen or fifteen. Since they had to be strong in later years, they had to prepare for the future. Old Indians believed that magic to make young men strong came from a plant known to them as *toloache*. To us it is known as Jimsonweed, a plant with huge white bell-like flowers. The root of the plant was chopped fine and mixed with water. All who drank of the mixture had dreams. It would kill anyone who drank very much of it. Older Indians watched to see that the young men drank just enough and no more.

Some coming-of-age ceremony for boys was held by almost all the tribes. Men from nearby villages brought their young boys and came to help in the ceremony. A brush fence was built in a large circle just outside the village. The men brought the boys to the center of this circle. The leader of the visiting tribe mixed the drink. Each boy took some of the bitter water. Then the men led them back into the village where the village people waited to greet them. A fire was built and as the men hummed and danced around the fire, the boys became sleepy. When they did, the men took them back to the circle outside the village. Here the boys were left to have their dreams. Perhaps some dreamed of hunting and killing a wild animal. Others may have dreamed of taking long journeys without getting tired. Words or songs may have come to them in their dreams that made them feel brave. Whatever the dream, it was believed that some day he would be able to do or to become what he had dreamed about.

After the dreams were over the older men came back. Boys told them about their wonderful dreams. Then the men sang to them and told them things they thought they should know. Some of the things they may have told the boys were: "The earth helps you. The sky sees what you do. Everyone will see that you are good if you do right. Right will always win out over wrong and good will always win out over evil. Believe these things. Tell them to your sons later. If you do, you will live long." These were the lessons taught to the young boys by the men of the tribe.

Then the men made sand paintings much like those made for

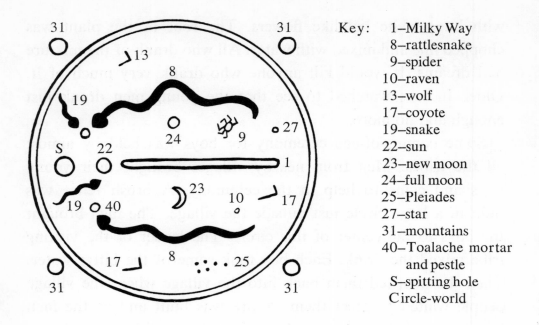

Key:
1–Milky Way
8–rattlesnake
9–spider
10–raven
13–wolf
17–coyote
19–snake
22–sun
23–new moon
24–full moon
25–Pleiades
27–star
31–mountains
40–Toalache mortar
   and pestle
S–spitting hole
Circle–world

A sand painting was made at both the boys' and girls' growing up-ceremonies.

the girls' ceremony. Boys chewed sage balls and dropped them into the sand painting. In this way they, too, became a part of the tribe and the world. The sand was swept away but the sage balls were taken by the men to a secret place and left there. The men said that the boys had now become men. They were ready to go hunting and fishing for the family's food.

The final test of manhood came when the boys were eighteen. After a night of dancing, the chief and older men took the young men outside the village. There they were led to a large nest of stinging ants. Each boy had to lie there and let the ants sting him. If he did this, he passed the test of bravery. "Never will the sting of an arrow hurt you," the older men said. More lessons were taught to them about rules of the tribe and about the work that they would have to do later. Not all tribes had this test but they had others to prove bravery. So passed from one age to another, the customs of these people.

Marriage

When he was ready to marry, the young man looked around for a girl who was good at gathering acorns and making baskets. No matter how she looked, he did not want a lazy wife. She did not have to be one of the girls in his own village or even from his own tribe. Marriage was often a matter of buying a bride. Robes of squirrel or deerskin, arrow points, skin, or strings of beads were given to the bride's parents as an offering for her. The young man who gave the most was able to get the girl he wanted for his wife. If he did not have enough gifts, he gave what he had and went to live with the bride's parents and worked for them to pay for the rest. In this way he not only paid for her but showed the parents that he was a good worker and able to care for his new wife. The marriage ceremony was a simple one. The medicine man decorated the girl with the finest feathers he had. Dancers circled around her as they sang

Miwok dance headdress.   *Yuki dance headdress.*

and told her that she must work hard, be honest and kind. Then all the villagers had a dance and a feast and the ceremony was over.

Death

An important ceremony was held when anyone in the tribe died. Neighboring tribes were invited to come. Some tribes buried their dead but many of them burned their dead. The house and part of the person's belongings were burned at the same time.

Certain tribes believed that a widow should cut or burn off her hair. She then had to put tar on her head and a "squaw cap" and leave it on for a year. She could not eat meat for a year either. Northern California women wore a mourning necklace made of bits of tar. Other widows made belts from their hair and wore them for a year.

The real mourning ceremony came about a year later. Before the ceremony little images were made out of grasses or cattails. Great care was used in making and dressing them. On the back of each one was put a little net with meal or a gift in it. These were for the journey to the "other world." At the ceremony songs were sung all night and in the morning there was feasting. As everyone sang, the family threw the images one by one into the fire. While this was going on there was mumbling and groaning. After the ceremony was over, the person was forgotten and his name was never spoken of again.

Eagle Ceremony

Another important ceremony was given in honor of the eagle. His feathers were much respected, for they were used for ceremonial clothes. There were those who believed that the eagle was in the world before people and that eagle feathers had a certain magic. They thought that once the eagle had flown north, south, east, and west. When he could not escape, he was willing to have people use his feathers for special occasions.

Eagle's nests were very valuable to a tribe and they were guarded closely. A chief would take the young eagles from the nests and keep them in his home. After the eagle was older, the feathers were ready to be plucked at a special ceremony. The chief called the people together and told them that it was time to send the eagle to the "other world." He said to the people, "Here is a messenger ready to go to the "other world."

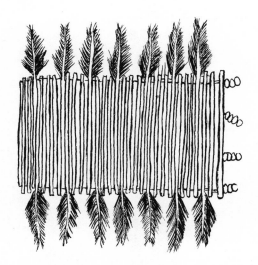

Dance headband worn by the Pomo.

Do you have any messages to go—either good or evil?" There was great mumbling among the people as they told their messages to the eagle. As the medicine man looked at the eagle with his piercing eyes, the eagle fell dead. Perhaps he choked the eagle but the people believed that it was his magic. The eagle's feathers were taken to be made into ceremonial skirts later. As for the eagle, he was cast into the fire so that he could go to the "other world" with the messages. Then men put on their eagle skirts and danced wildly in a circle. As they did, the feathers spread out wide around them and seemed to soar as the eagle had once done.

The Swordfish Dance

Canaliño Indians thought that the swordfish was a very special friend of their tribe. They were certain that it was the swordfish that drove whales to the shore where they could be caught for food. Whenever a whale washed up on the beach, the village people had plenty to eat for weeks. The Canaliño had a swordfish dance in which they wore a scaly headdress that looked like the head of the swordfish (such a headdress has been found in a Canaliño grave). As the Indians danced they gave thanks to the swordfish for his kindness. They probably asked that more whales be sent to the shore!

Exhibit showing Swordfish Ceremony. (Santa Barbara Museum of Natural History—Bosworth Lemere Photo)

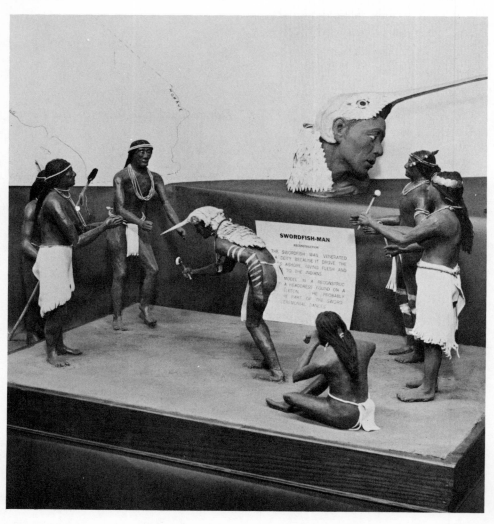

14   ONCE UPON A TIME
INDIAN TALES

INDIANS had many stories about the world in which they lived and the other "spirit world." Their stories told of the eagle, so important and the coyote, so clever and cunning. They wanted so much to know how the world was made, about thunder and lightning, earthquakes and everything else around them. Because they could not understand all these things they made up stories about them. These stories were told from father to son and from one tribe to another until at last they seemed to be true.

HOW MAN WAS MADE

One of the tales was about Coyote, who wished to make men on earth. All the animals were called together so Coyote could get their advice as to how this could be done. "Let man have a voice that can roar and sharp teeth and claws. Then he can scare other animals," said the Lion. Grizzly Bear did not agree. He thought it much more important that man be very strong. Deer thought that man should have beautiful long horns. Mountain Sheep said that if he had horns they would get caught in the bushes. "His horns should be rolled up like mine," said the Mountain Sheep. The Owl thought that man should have wings and the Mouse thought he should have sharp eyes so that he could see what he was eating.

Coyote listened to what they told him. "All of you are foolish animals for all of you want man to be like yourselves. Man should be all of the things you say but he should be as wise as I am!" Thus spoke the Coyote.

Finally, the animals set to work to make man out of lumps of clay. Each worked to make man look like himself until each one grew so tired that he fell asleep. Wise old Coyote stayed awake and decided that he would fool the other animals. While they were asleep he threw water on their clay until it melted away. By morning when the animals awakened, the Coyote had made man. He made him just the way that he thought he should be—the best part of each of the animals. Thus man was made by Coyote.

—YOKUTS LEGEND

HOW FIRE AND LIGHT CAME TO THE NEW LAND

After the people and the land were made, Mr. Lizard found it to be a cold and dark place. There was no light; no fire to make him warm. So he sent his friend, little white-footed Mouse to a faraway land to steal fire. The Mouse stole the fire and hurried away with it as fast as he could. Just then he heard someone running after him. He hid his bright spark of fire in the cedar and buckeye trees nearby. Suddenly there was a great

Suddenly a great fire blazed up. (United States Forest Service)

burst of fire in the trees. It seemed to blaze up as high as the sky! From this came the sun—warm and bright and in this way, light came to the New Land.

Not all the trees caught on fire and flamed so high. Some of the fire was so covered with branches that it only smoked. Since then, men have been able to rub twigs together and the fire comes to life all over again.

STORY OF EL CAPITAN IN YOSEMITE VALLEY

Many long years ago two little boys went out to play in a grassy valley (which the Indians call *Ahwahnee*). They splashed and swam in the stream that ran through the valley until they were tired out. Then they climbed onto a large rock and fell asleep. No sooner had they done so than the rock on which they were lying began to grow. In those days the Indians thought that rocks did this. The rock grew higher and higher—up and up—until it seemed to touch the sky. Still the boys slept on.

Their mother called to her children but there was no answer. She called the animals together and asked them to help her find the boys. The animals told her about the children on the rock and what must have happened. All of them wondered how they could get the boys down. One by one each animal tried to climb up the face of the rock but failed. About that time along came a little measuring worm. He was the kind of worm that traveled very slowly but very surely. The animals asked him if he would crawl up the big rock and he said that he would try. Slowly, ever so slowly, inch by inch, he edged up and up and up! Soon the tiny worm was so high that no one could see him any more.

The mother and the animals waited for a very long time at the foot of the mighty cliff that was nearly a mile high. They did not know it but the little worm had not given up. At last he reached the top of the stony cliff where the boys were sleeping. The measuring worm awakened them and slowly brought them safely down to their mother.

In later years, this huge rocky cliff was given the name El Capitan.

HOW THE PEOPLE LEARNED

The New People made by Coyote found that the land was fair and that there was plenty of food. Men learned to live by watching to see how the animals lived. They went into the woods and found food that was good to eat. From the Crane they learned to spear and eat fish. From Trout they learned how to swim. Deer taught them how to run fast. Ants taught that much could be done by working together. Birds, with their happy songs, taught them that there was joy in the world. Indian

The rock that grew and grew—El Capitan, Yosemite National Park. (Hubert A. Lowman)

women watched the birds build their nests, and from this they learned how to weave baskets.

From all the creatures, great and small, the people learned how to live in the New Land. They grew in numbers and became strong. The people looked at the Sun and gave thanks for its light and warmth and for making things grow. They danced to give thanks to the One who had made them and the world they lived in.

An Indian storage basket for piñon nuts made like a bird's nest. (Hubert A. Lowman)

15 WHAT BECAME OF THE INDIANS

WE LEARNED in the beginning about the first explorers who came to California and brought back reports of seeing Indians living along the coast. Each time the explorers came, the Indians must have wondered why they came and what would happen next. As we found out, there were no explorers for over a hundred and sixty years. Indians kept on living in the same ways they had always known.

Then there was interest in California all over again. Russian ships had landed on the north coast of America. They found it to be a good place for hunting. On the islands were otters and seals, the skins of which made fine warm coats. People of cold lands were glad to pay high prices for such furs. The Russians kept coming nearer and nearer to California. News about this went back to Spain. Spain had also heard about other countries that had become interested in California. Now Spain saw that something had to be done quickly to keep the land once claimed for her by the early Spanish explorers.

Spain knew that the Indians living in California would have to be taught to be friendly before anything else could be done. At the time, Father Junípero Serra was president of the Lower California missions and, as such, had worked with and taught the people there. He had heard of California and had always wanted to go there. He was delighted when told that he had been chosen to work with the California Indians.

Gaspar de Portolá, the Spanish governor of Lower California, was chosen to head a party of soldiers into California. The plan was to build *presidios* or forts along the coast where the soldiers could live. They would protect Spain's right to California and would drive out any other countries that tried to claim it.

After the *presidios,* Father Serra was to direct the building of the missions. Each mission was to have a church or chapel, workshops, and places for the Indians to live. Indians were to leave their homes, help build missions, and then live and work in the missions. They were to help the padres grow crops, learn about the Christian religion, and live in all ways as they were taught. It was expected that the mission would become the church in a town or *pueblo* that would grow up around it. It was expected that this plan would take many years. By that time, it was believed that the Indians would be able to take care of themselves. Mission lands would be given to them and they could grow their own crops and live in the new ways taught to them by the padres.

Fifty-four years passed by (1769 to 1823). Indians did build missions, twenty-one of them from the south to the north of California.* Missions became their homes, their new way of life. Thousands of adobes were made by Indian hands; irrigation ditches for bringing water to the missions were built. Indians learned to make many useful things in the mission workshops. Women did the cooking and weaving. Most important to the padres was that the Indians learned a new language (Spanish)

* See Bauer, *California Mission Days.*

and a new religion. Life at the missions gave them food and a place to eat but Indians who had been free for so many years sometimes ran away. As a rule they returned before soldiers caught them and brought them back to the missions. There were many hard years but as time went on the mission lands grew larger and richer. These were important days in California's history.

Then a change came on April 11, 1822 when the Mexican Empire flag was raised at the Presidio of Monterey, California. News soon spread that California no longer belonged to Spain but to Mexico. In 1834 word came from Mexico that the missions were no longer needed and would be closed. Padres left and went to live in Spain, Mexico, and to the Santa Barbara Mission. Some of the mission lands were given to the Indians as had been planned. However, the Indians had not learned

Adobe bricks made by Indians were used to build mission walls. (Arthur Barr Productions, Inc.) From Bauer: California Mission Days

enough to care for themselves or for the land given them; so they drifted away to other places. Gradually almost all the mission lands were broken up into *ranchos,* and *rancheros* became the new owners.[†]

What were the Indians to do? They had to go to work on the new *ranchos* or go back to the places they had once lived. Some who knew how to farm and care for cattle went to live on the *ranchos.* For years many of the misson Indians were the chief workers on the *ranchos.* Indian women worked in *rancho* homes and cared for the *ranchero's* children. Finally they grew tired of this kind of life and hundreds of them went back to their old homes in the valleys and mountains. Many died from diseases they had never had nor ever heard of before.

Other changes were ahead for the Indians and for all of the Californians. Mexico and the United States both wanted California. On January 13, 1847, they signed a paper that ended California's part in the Mexican War. This was the beginning of American California. One year later, in February 1848, the United States made peace with Mexico. It was not until September 9, 1850 that California was made the thirty-first state of the United States.

When all this was happening, gold was found at Coloma on the South Fork of the American River.[‡] From all over the world, people rushed to find gold in California. These were important years in California's history but it was a sad time for the Indians. Gold meant little to them for their needs were few. They could not understand what was going on and so they went further and further back into the mountains. Oak trees that had once given them acorns for food were cut down. People by the hundreds looked for gold in rivers and streams. Where towns sprang up there was no room for Indian villages. Even in places where miners did not go, small groups of Indians stayed for awhile and then moved on. There seemed to be no place for the Indi-

[†] See Bauer, *California Rancho Days.*
[‡] See Bauer, *California Gold Days.*

124

Indians went to work on the ranchos. (Arthur Barr Productions, Inc.)
From Bauer: California Rancho Days

ans. By this time they were poor and not able to take care of themselves as they had once done. Once they had found enough to eat; now many of them starved. Many fell ill and died. Most of them had been honest and peaceful. Now some of them stole horses, food, and other things and fought to keep strangers away from their part of the land. Many of the Indians were hunted down and shot.

Year after year the Indians lost more and more of the land that had once belonged to them. Finally, in the early 1850s, the United States set aside certain lands for them called reservations. The idea was to get the Indians out of the white man's way and to give them land for their new homes. After a period of time they seemed to become used to the new way of life. At least they had places they could call their own and they did not

Present-day reservation Indian boy beside rock where acorns were once pounded into meal. (Hubert A. Lowman)

have to pay taxes on their land. They could live with their relatives and friends.

Through the years since then, Indians have married into other races. There are those who have not but many now belong to mixed races. Very few speak an Indian language any more. Middle-aged Indians usually speak only Spanish and English; younger people know only English.

There are 117 reservations in California, but most of them are very small. On sixteen of the reservations, Indians have been given land which can be passed on to their children. On other reservations the land can be used but not owned. There are no

Mission Indians left but some still live where once there was mission land. The largest reservation in California is the Hoopa Valley Reservation in the northwest part of the state (Humboldt County). Over nine hundred Indians live here along the Trinity River. South of the Hoopa Reservation is the Round Valley Reservation, where a few Indians from several different tribes live.*

Only bits of the old Indian life remain. Each year there seems to be less and less. Not many Indians in California even know the plants once used for food. They do not know most of the old stories that once were told so many times. Few women make the beautiful baskets any more. Materials for them are hard to find and it seems to be too much work to make them. Some of the older Indian men (especially in the Hoopa Valley area) remember some of the old-time ceremonies. Some of the younger men still do the White Deerskin dances. They still do the Jump Dance, in which treasures such as obsidian pieces and beautiful ornaments are shown. Headdresses for the Jump Dances are bands of redheaded woodpecker scalps and hummingbird's feathers.

In San Diego County, at the foot of Mount Palomar (where the world's largest telescope is located), there is a church built by and for the Luiseño Indians. It is the only church left from mission days where Indians still go to church services. Every year in June, the Pala Indians have a celebration in which they march with banners and lighted torches. They have a dinner for their friends and a program of Indian and Mexican dances, games, and songs. The Luiseño still have a chief and a clothes-burning ceremony is held whenever one of their tribe dies.

Most Indians do not live on reservations but in towns and cities. They have become a part of the life around them; they are citizens and may vote. Some live in the country and the government has helped them with their farming. Some Indians help farmers pick fruit and harvest crops. Between seasons, they

* See Addendum: "Where the Indians Are Today" and map location of California Indian reservations.

care for their own orchards, fields, and cattle. Those who live in cities have their own homes and cars and live as any other working people do. They work in offices, factories, and trades, and attend public schools. Very valuable property is owned by certain Indians such as the Cahuilla (*Agua Caliente*) in the Palm Springs area. About one hundred Indians own property in that area worth millions of dollars.

Studies are being made by the United States government to work out the Indian's problems. The government is trying to plan toward a time when Indians will own the land on which they live. There may come a time when there will be no Indian reservations.

No matter what the future may bring, there are some things that can never take the place of the peaceful, easygoing life of the Indian days of long ago. Even though the old Indian days and ways are almost gone, the story of that part of California's history should be remembered.

The church at Pala, built by the Luiseños, is the only church left from mission days which is still attended by Indians. (Hubert A. Lowman)

ADDENDA

IN WHAT FORMER INDIAN TERRITORY
DO YOU LIVE TODAY?

In most cases the Indian villages were not located within the boundaries of present-day cities or else there were many small villages clustered in or around the sites of present California cities.

INDIAN VILLAGES WERE LOCATED ON THE SAME SITE OF (OR NEAR) THESE PRESENT CITIES

PRESENT CITY	INDIAN VILLAGE OR VILLAGES	PRESENT CITY	INDIAN VILLAGE OR VILLAGES
Auburn	Hangwite	Rendondo Beach	Engva
Azusa	Asuksa	Sacramento	Singawü-nu
Bakersfield	Woilo	St. Helena	Anakota-Noma
Calistoga	Nihletk-sonoma	Salinas	Saho-n
Carpinteria	Michopshdo,	San Diego	Pushuni
Chico	Kolok	San Fernando	Pasek
Colfax	Umucha	San Francisco	Siba
Colton	Takema	(See below)	
	Wacha-Vak	San Gabriel	Orolso-n
Escondido	Mehelom-Pom-Pauvo	San Jose	Matala-n
Fort Ross	Meteni	San Mateo	Teshaya
Fresno	Wakichi	San Miguel	Masau
Gaviota	Mich'lyu	San Pedro	Siuhtun,
Goleta	Heliok, Paltocac	Santa Barbara	Alpincha
Grass Valley	Tipotoya	Santa Clara	Tanaiu
Hollister	Mutsun	Santa Cruz	Sokel
Hueneme	Weneme	Santa Maria	Nipomo
Jackson	Tukupe-sü	Santa Monica	Mupu
Knights Landing	Vodol	(See below)	
Lakeport	Kashibadon	Santa Paula	Satikoi
Lompoc	Lompoc	Saticoy	Kashtuk
Long Beach	Shua	Saugus	Liwanelowa
Los Alamos	Masuwuk	Sausalito	Batiklechawi
Los Angeles	Wenot, Yangna	Sebastopol	Sekspe
Mariposa	Kasumati	Sespe	Shimiyi
Martinez	Saklan	Simi	Huchi
Marysville	Humata	Sonoma	Kuluti
Mendocino	Buldam	Sonora	Vulyul,
Mesa Grande	Tukumak	Suisun City	Nesala
Monterey	Tamo-tk	Temecula	Temeku
Monticello	Topaidi-hi	Ventura	Lolop
Mugu, Point	Wihachet	Visalia	Yokodo
Napa	Tulukai	Yosemite	Awani
Novato	Chokeche	Yountville	Kalmus
Ojai	Ahwat	San Francisco	Awas-te
Oroville	Apautawilü	Santa Monica	Sa'an
Paso Robles	Cholame		
Petaluma	Meleya		
Piru	Pi'idhuku		
Placerville	Poktono, Pota		
Pomona	Toibi		
Porterville	Chokowisho, Koyeti		

CALIFORNIA PLACE NAMES LEFT BY THE INDIANS

The Indians left their place names scattered thickly over the map of California; names of counties, cities, mountains, rivers, and valleys. Californians are apt to take place names for granted but the names had meanings to those of other days. We know that California has many Spanish place names and we understand many of them. We are not apt to know Indian names when we see them. Even when we do, we do not usually know what the name means. Much of this part of our history has been lost.

There are nine counties in the state that have Indian names: Colusa, Modoc, Mono, Napa, Shasta, Tehama, Tuolumne, Yolo, and Yuba. Two others, Inyo and Siskiyou, are supposed to be Indian. We do not know the meanings of any of the above names. We know that Indians usually did not use the names of people for places. Words they used were usually about something that happened or the place where it happened, such as "clover valley," "red rock," "snow mountains," or "bear place." Check the names below and perhaps you will find Indian place names in the area where you live.

NAME	MEANING	COUNTY
Aguanga	Luiseño village name	Riverside
Ahwahnee	Miwok village in Yosemite Valley	Madera
Anacapa (Island)	Chumash name	Ventura
Azusa	Gabrieleño, "skunk place"	Los Angeles
Cabazon	Cahuilla Indian chief	Riverside
Cahuenga (Pass)	Gabrieleño name	Los Angeles
Cajalco	Cahuilla, "gathering place of waters"	Riverside
Calabasas	Chumash, "place of wild goose"	Los Angeles
Calpella	Indian chief (culpalan), "shellfish bearer"	Mendocino
Camulos	Chumash, "a fruit"	Ventura
Carquinez (Strait)	Wintun village	Contra Costa
Castaic	Shoshonean, "our eyes"	Los Angeles
Chemehuevi (Mts.)	Name of tribe	San Bernardino
Cholame	Salinan Indian village	San Luis Obispo
Chowchilla	Yokut, "murderers"	Madera
Coahuila	Probably Cahuilla tribe	Riverside
Coalinga	"place of coal"	Fresno
Cohasset	Algonkian, Koowas—"pines" and "it" or "pines place"	Butte
Coloma	Maidu village	El Dorado
Colusa	Wintun village	Colusa
Cucamonga	Gabrieleño village	San Bernardino
Cuyamaca	"rain yonder"	San Diego
Gualala	Pomo, "meeting place of waters"	Mendocino
Hemet	Luiseño "corn valley"	Riverside

NAME	MEANING	COUNTY
Hetch-Hetchy (Valley)	Miwok, name of plant that bears edible seeds	Tuolumne
Hoopa (Hupa)	Yurok, Indian name of the valley	Humboldt
Hueneme	Chumash, "place of security"	Ventura
Inyo (County)	Shoshonean, an Indian tribe	Inyo
Jacumba	Digueño, "hut by the water"	San Diego
Jalama	Name of Chumash village, meaning unknown	Santa Barbara
Jamacao	Diegueño, "wild squash plant"	San Diego
Jamul	Diegueño "foam"	San Diego
Jolon	Salinan village	Monterey
Kaweah	Yokut word, meaning unknown	Tulare
Klamath	Klamath name, perhaps "people"	Del Norte
Lompoc	Chumash, "little lake" or "little lagoon"	Santa Barbara
Malibu	Chumash village, "Maliwu"	Los Angeles

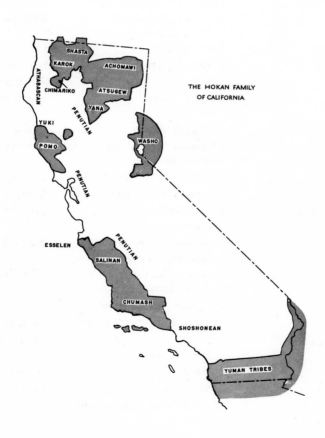

THE HOKAN FAMILY
OF CALIFORNIA

NAME	MEANING	COUNTY
Marin (County)	Probably Spanish word for Coast Miwok headman	Marin
Matilija	Chumash village name	Ventura
Modoc (County)	Lutuami name for "south"	Modoc
Mojave	Mohave name for their tribe	Kern
Mokelumne Hill	Miwok village, name said to mean "people of Mokel"	Calaveras
Mono (County)	Yokut name for branch of Shoshoneans	Mono
Morongo (Valley)	"serrano," "meadow"	San Bernardino
Mugu (Point)	Chumash, "beach"	Ventura
Napa	Pomo name for "harpoon point"	Napa
Natoma	Maidu, "upstream"	Sacramento
Nipomo	Chumash village	San Luis Obispo
Noyo	Pomo village name, meaning unknown	Mendocino
Ojai	Chumash, "moon"	Ventura
Olancha	Yokut tribe or village	Inyo
Pacoima	Gabrieleño place name	Los Angeles
Pala	Luiseño "water"	San Diego
Petaluma	Coast Miwok, "flat-back"	Sonoma
Piru	Shoshonean name of a Chumash village, "plant" or "grass"	Ventura
Pismo Beach	Chumash name	San Luis Obispo
Piute	Shoshonean, "water Ute"	San Bernardino
Poway	Luiseño, "meeting of the valleys"	San Diego
Saticoy	Chumash village	Ventura
Sespe	Chumash village name, said to mean "fish"	Ventura
Shasta (City)	Name of Shasta headman?	Shasta
Simi	Chumash place name	Ventura
Siskiyou (County)	Indian word, meaning unknown	Siskiyou
Sisquoc	Chumash village name, meaning unknown	Santa Barbara
Soboba (Hot Springs)	Indian village name, meaning unknown	Riverside
Somis	Chumash village name	Ventura
Sonoma	Wappo word, "village of"	Sonoma
Stanilaus (County)	Chief of Consumnes or "earth village"	Stanilaus
Suisun	Wintun village name	Solano
Tahoe (City)	Washo, "big water" (Taa-oo)	Placer
Tamalpais (Mt.)	Coast Miwok, "bay mountain"	Marin

NAME	MEANING	COUNTY
Tehachapi	Shoshonean, "land of acorns"	Kern
Tehama	Wintun Village	Tehama
Temecula	Luiseño, "sun"	Riverside
Tomales (Bay)	Coast Miwok, "bay" (tamal)	Marin
Topanga	Gabrieleño place name	Los Angeles
Topock	Mohave, "bridge"	San Bernardino
Tuolumne (County)	Miwok or Yokut (unknown)	Tuolumne
Tujunga	Gabrieleño village	Los Angeles
Ukiah	Pomo, "south valley"	Mendocino
Weott	Wyot place name	Humboldt
Yolo	South Wintun, "place of the rushes"	Yolo
Yosemite	Indian village, "grizzly bear" perhaps	Mariposa
Yreka	Indian name for Mount Shasta (I-e-ka)	Siskiyou
Yucaipa	Shoshean village name	San Bernardino

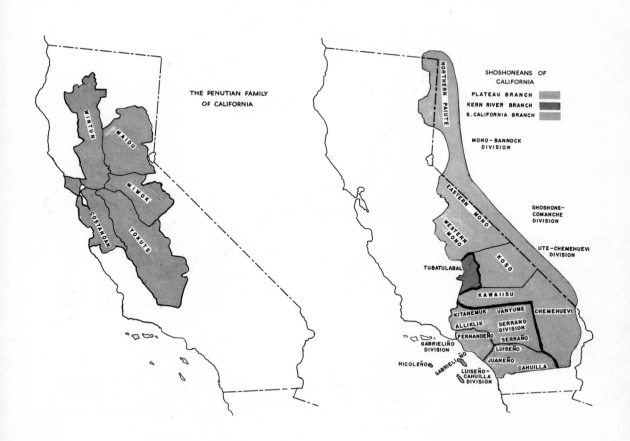

THE PENUTIAN FAMILY
OF CALIFORNIA

WINTUN
MAIDU
MIWOK
COSTANOAN
YOKUTS

SHOSHONEANS OF
CALIFORNIA

PLATEAU BRANCH
KERN RIVER BRANCH
S. CALIFORNIA BRANCH

NORTHERN PAIUTE

MONO-BANNOCK
DIVISION

EASTERN MONO

WESTERN MONO

KOSO

SHOSHONE-
COMANCHE
DIVISION

UTE-CHEMEHUEVI
DIVISION

TUBATULABAL

KAWAIISU

KITANEMUK   VANYUME   CHEMEHUEVI

ALLIKLIK   SERRANO
DIVISION

FERNANDEÑO   SERRAÑO

GABRIELIÑO
DIVISION   LUISEÑO

NICOLEÑO   JUANEÑO

GABRIELIÑO   CAHUILLA

LUISEÑO-
CAHUILLA
DIVISION

WHERE THE INDIANS ARE TODAY*

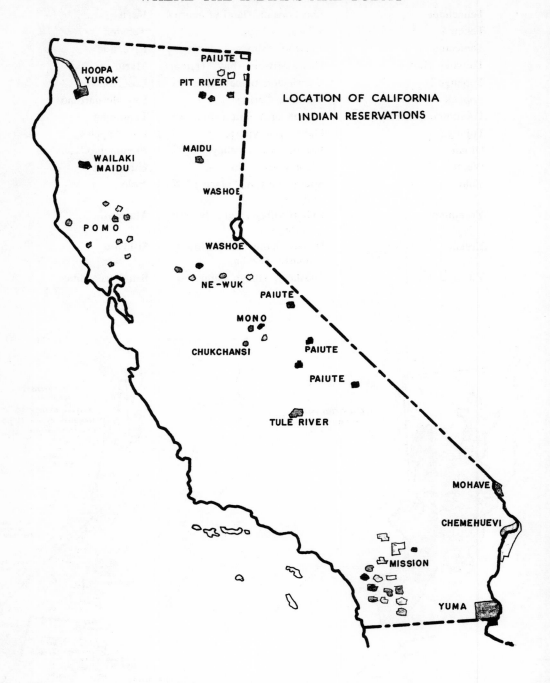

LOCATION OF CALIFORNIA
INDIAN RESERVATIONS

Except for a few reservations shown on the map, there are no large Indian settlements or land holdings in California. There are about 117 small reservations and rancherías. Many Indians live on their own homesites, especially in southern California (Riverside and San Diego Counties).

1)	FORT YUMA RESERVATION—Winterhaven (southeast area of California)	9141 acres
2)	HOOPA VALLEY—Hoopa (northwest area of California)	86,277 acres
3)	HOOPA VALLEY EXTENSION, Weitchpec	7092 acres
4)	PALM SPRINGS (AGUA CALIENTE) RESERVATION— Palm Springs (southern California)	29,967 acres
5)	TULE RIVER RESERVATION—Porterville (Tulare County)	54,116 acres
		186,593 acres

*United States Department of the Interior
Geographic Survey, Washington, D.C., 1961*

THE 1960 UNITED STATES CENSUS:

39,014 Indians living in California (mostly in Los Angeles, Humboldt, and San Diego Counties). This total Indian population of the state includes Indians who have come to live in California from other states.

7,618 California Indians living either on or near Indian Reservations in California.

INDIAN CALENDAR

Those were the days when time did not stand still but there were no calendars and no clocks. No one knew his exact age. Most groups did not even have a word for "year" but used the word "world" instead. At the end of the cold season, an Indian might have said, "the world went," meaning that the cold time was over.

Probably every group, however, had its own way of telling time during the year. The Maidu knew twelve moons, beginning in the spring season. The Yurok calendar counted moons beginning with the middle of winter. Some could tell the time of the year by the stars. Some put knots in a string to count the days. Nature told the time of the year by when different foods were ready to be gathered. Indians knew exactly which foods ripened in each season. Each month had a certain meaning to these people. A sample of this is found in the Pomo group.

POMO CALENDAR

January	Buckeyes ripen	July	Manzanita ripens
February	Cold winds blow	August	Acorns appear
March	Growth begins	September	Soaproot dug
April	Flowers begin to bloom	October	Trees cut down
May	Seeds ripen	November	Cold begins
June	Bulbs mature	December	Leaves yellow and fall

HOW TO PRONOUNCE WORDS

Consonants are pronounced somewhat as in English. The vowels are pronounced as follows:

a	as in father	(ah)
e	as in they	(ā)
i	as in marine	(ē)
o	as in note	(ō)
u	as in flute	(oo)
ai	as in fire	(ī)
au	as in now	(au)

adobe	ah-doh'-bay	unburned brick dried in the sun
agave	ah-gah'-vay	plant used for food
asphalt	as'-fawlt	black, tar-like substance
Bahia de las Fumas	Bah-hee'-ah deh lahs Foo'-mahs	Bay of Smokes (near present-day Ventura)
balsa	bahl'-sah	boat made of tule reeds
Cabrillo, Juan Rodríquez	Cahb-reel'-yo, Hwahn Rohd-ree'-gays	Portuguese explorer
cactus	kak'-tus	thorny plant used for food
Carpinteria	Car-peen-ter-ee'-ah	city in Santa Barbara County; means "carpenter shop"
chia	chee'-ah	a kind of sage
Colorado	Koh-loh-rah'-doh	Indians lived near the Colorado River. Means "red" in Spanish
Concepción (Point)	Kohn-sep-see-o'hn	point on California coast
corral	koh-rahl'	pen for animals
coyote	ki-oh'-tee	wild animal
dentalium	den-tay'-lee-uhm	a tooth-like shell used for Indian money
Diomedes	Di-oh-mee'-dees	islands in the Bering Strait
Ferrelo, Bartolomeo	Fay-ray'-lo, Bahr-toh'-lo-may-oh	Spanish explorer
Goleta	Goh-lay'-tah	city in California; means "schooner"
islay (or yslay)	ees'-lay	Indian name for wild plums
Junípero Serra	Hoo-nee'-pay-roh Say'-rah	founder of the first nine missions in California
La Victoria	Lah Veec-toh'-reeah	one of Cabrillo's ships
magnesite	mag'-nee-site	a mineral
mano	mah'-no	stone used in grinding on a metate
manzanita	mahn-zhan-nee'-tah	a shrub
mesquite	mehs-keet'	plant with bean-like pods
metate	may-tah'-tay	stone slab used in grinding
moccasin	moc'-kah-zhin or moc'-ah-sin	shoe made of leather

138

Monterey	Mohn-tay-ray'	city in California
mortar	mohr'-tar	bowl used in pounding
obsidian	ob-seh'-dee-ahn	a volcanic glass
olivella	ohl-ee-veh'-lah	shell used for beads by the Indians
padre	pah'-dray	priest or friar
pestle	pes'-ehl	used to pound acorns and seeds in a mortar
Portolá, Gaspar de	Por-toh-lah', Gahs'-pahr day	lead first party of soldiers into California
presidio	pray-see'-dee-oh	fort, place where the soldiers lived
pueblo	pway'-blow	town or village
rancheria	rahn-chay-ree'-ah	name given to Indian village
ranchero	rahn-chay'-ro	owner of a ranch
rancho	rahn'-cho	land granted by the Spanish and Mexican governments
Sacramento	Sah-krah-mehn'-toh	capital of California, means sacrament
San Antonio (Mount)	Sahn Ahn-toh'-nee-oh	mountain peak
San Diego	Sahn Dee-ay'-go	city in California
San Fernando	Sahn Fer-nahn'-do	city in California
San Francisco	Sahn Frahn-sees'-co	city in California
San Gabriel	Sahn Gahb'-ree-ehl	city in California
San Gorgonio (Mount)	Sahn Gor-gohn'-ee-oh	mountain peak
San Joaquin	Sahn Ho-ah-keen'	valley in California
San Juan Capistrano	Sahn Hwahn Kah-pees-trahn'-o	city in California
San Luis Obispo	Sahn Lwees Oh-bees'-po	city in California
San Miquel (Island)	Sahn Mee-goo-ehl'	one of the Santa Barbara Channel islands
San Pedro	Sahn Pay'-droh	city in California
San Salvador	Sahn Sahl'-vah-door	one of Cabrillo's ships
Santa Barbara	Sahn'-tah Bahr'-Bahr-ah	city in California
Santa Catalina (Island)	Sahn'-tah Kah-tah-leen'-ah	island
Santa Rosa	Sahn'-tah Roh'-sah	city in California
shaman	shah'-man	medicine man (or woman)
Shasta (Mount)	Shas'-tah	California mountain peak
Sierra Nevada	See-ehr'-rah Nay-vah'-dah	mountain range
steatite	stee'-ah-tite	soapstone used by Indians for bowls, charmstones, etc.
temescal	tay-mehs'-cahl	sweat house
tomolo	toh'-moh-loh	plank canoe
totolache	toh-toh-lah'-chee	jimsonweed used in boys' growing-up ceremony
toyon	toh'-yohn	shrub with red berries (Christmas berries)
tule	too'-lay	reed found in marshy land
Ventura	Vehn-too'-rah	city in California
yucca	yuc'-ah	plant used as a food

CHART OF TRIBES

TRIBE (Family)	TERRITORY	CLOTHES AND ORNAMENTS	HOUSES
TOLOWA (Athabascan)	Smith River, Del Norte County, close to Oregon.		
HUPA (Athabascan)	Trinity River.		
CHILULA (Athabascan)	Lower Redwood Creek, along redwood belt to a few miles above Minor Creek.		Had plank houses.
WHILKUT (Athabascan)	Redwood Creek above Chilula and Mad River, wedged in between Wiyot and Wintun.		Bark slab houses. The sweat house was earth-covered as in central California.
MATTOLE (Athabascan)	Cape Mendocino by Bear River, Mattole River, and few miles of Eel River.		
NONGATL (Athabascan)	Along Eel River, creeks in area, and upper waters of Mad River.		
SINKYONE (Athabascan)	South Fork—Eel River and coast above Shelter Cove to point between Usal and Rockport (next to Coast. Yuki)	Used yellow-hammer feather headbands as in central California.	Cone-shaped and made of bark slabs.
LASSIK (Athabascan)	Few miles above mouth of South Fork and to head of Mad. River		Same as Sinkyone.
KATO "lake" (Athabascan)	Northernmost courses of South Fork of Eel River.		

140

This chart indicates some of the main differences among the various Indian tribes. Blank spaces have been left where the things they made and their customs were alike and are described elsewhere in the book.

FOOD	BASKETS	BOATS	CUSTOMS AND OTHER INFORMATION
		Redwood dugout canoes, twice as long as any other tribe had.	Much like Yurok and Hupa.
			Traded with the Yurok. Gave animal skins and inland foods for redwood canoes and seafoods.
		No boats.	Little known about them.
	Very few baskets.		
	Some baskets but not too well made.		Ceremonies few and simple. They were considered a poor tribe.
			Caught deer by driving them into corrals made of logs.
			Redwood country. Nearly fifty villages; some still left at Round Valley reservation (others near Laytonville). Had customs like Yuki but Kato and Yuki had quarrels. Women smeared black pitch on face if there was a death in the family.

TRIBE (Family)	TERRITORY	CLOTHES AND ORNAMENTS	HOUSES
WAILAKI "north language" (Athabascan)	On Eel River furthest north.		
YUROK (Algonkin)	Along Klamath River.	Haliotis shells on fringes of women's aprons. Wore many ornaments. Women parted hair, bound like clubs, over each shoulder. On special occasions added fur or woodpecker scalps to hair style. Widows cut hair very short.	Redwood plank and the more ridges, the richer the person was supposed to be. Hard earthen floors.
WIYOT (Algonkin)	Lower Mad River, Humboldt Bay, and lower Eel River, mostly redwood forest land. Villages by stream, bay, or tidewater. Ocean front low and sandy.		
HUCHNON "mountain people" (Yukian)	Redwood valley near one of sources of Russian River, valley of the South Eel.		

FOOD	BASKETS	BOATS	CUSTOMS AND OTHER INFORMATION
Were great hunters. Caught elk and deer by running them down. Also did well in fishing.			More Athabascans here than any other part of the state except Hoopa (Hupa) Valley.
Ate more salmon than others. Better food than many tribes. Had fancy company spoons and many more utensils than others.	Flat basket caps. Conical carrying baskets. Used very large storage baskets. Large flat baskets for deer meat. Large ones for washing hands after feasts.	Dugout redwood log boats. Sold them to Hupa and Karok tribes. Used them mostly on rivers.	Had no chief. Yurok wanted very much to be rich. Were not warlike. If any damage, they paid for it; if anyone killed, family of deceased was paid. Had unusual chisel-like tool, a blade lashed to stone handle. Only Yurok had this kind. Used no rattles in their music or ceremonies. Had no Girls' Ceremony but when five years old, girls were tattooed with a black stripe from corner of mouth to below the chin. Tribe had sharp obsidian arrow points. Men had great speed in running. As they ran they prayed to sun and moon in singsong way. Yurok were outdoor people and loved all of nature.
		Canoes much like Yurok.	Shaman were women; received their power on mountaintops at night. They had headbands from which hung two strings of feathers.
			Called the "Redwoods people" by white men. Were friendly with the Pomo; hunted, fished, and traded with them. The Huchnon were very religious like the Yuki. During Boys' Ceremony the Pomo and Kato joined in ceremony with their boys.

TRIBE (Family)	TERRITORY	CLOTHES AND ORNAMENTS	HOUSES
COAST YUKI (Yukian)	Along coast between Kato and Pomo territories.		Cone-shaped bark house with steep roof.
YUKI (Yukian)	Along Coast Range Mts. All land lying in drainage of Eel River above the North Fork except along South Eel River.	Men wore string head nets. Women tattooed chins only.	Cone-shaped and earth-covered. Short, low entrance. Took two days to build; lasted about two years.
WAPPO "brave" (Yukian)	Held territory north of Sonoma Creek; valley of Napa River.		
MODOC (Lutamian)	Northern border of the state.	Wore tule leggings to the knee. Shredded tule blanket worn by women. Used snowshoes in winter.	Underground earth-covered brush house. Used steam not fire in sweat house.
ACHOMAWI (Hokan)	Pit River area (a stream people).	Deerskins used. Cut hole in middle, slipped over head. Skin sewed together at side seams.	Bark house, entered from the roof.

FOOD	BASKETS	BOATS	CUSTOMS AND OTHER INFORMATION
Salmon swimming upstream speared with two-pronged harpoons. Salmon swimming downstream caught with nets. Caught surf fish in net.	Made string from fibers of iris leaves.		Probably part of Huchnon, not Yuki family. Friendly with all their neighbors even though Yuki warred with the Kato. They wrapped their dead in deerskin or bear skins.
	Coiled baskets woven from right to left, unlike most tribes who wove from left to right. Made some baskets as flat as plates and some tiny ones for gifts or to hold some treasure. No basket caps worn by women.		A short people but had longest heads of any tribe. Had chiefs in large villages only. Yuki rarely went to the coast. Warlike and fought all their neighbors at various times. Had many ceremonies. Counted spaces between fingers (4), not fingers (5), and so counted by 8's (spaces between the two hands), not 10's (fingers). Rich man was called a "person man" —a man who was a real person. Chief was rich, friendly, and always ready to help. Richer people paid for a wife; wife's parents made a return in gifts. No mourning ceremony. Usually buried in large baskets along with some of the person's property.
			Language much like Pomo. Many low mountains in their territory but they were a valley people.
No acorns. Ate mostly meat, fish, and water-lily seeds.	Twined, soft baskets of tule with porcupine quills. Put design both outside and inside.	Dugout canoe and tule canoes. Tule ones when hunting and warfare, paddled with their hands.	More warlike than other tribes. Band bound around baby's head to make it high and narrow. Used board cradles for babies.
Not many acorns. Caught deer in deer pits. Pit River got its name from the deer pits in the area.	Twined soft baskets; not too well made.	Dug out pine or cedar.	Few ceremonies. Buried dead in basket in sitting-up position. Widow cut off hair and made belt of it.

TRIBE (Family)	TERRITORY	CLOTHES AND ORNAMENTS	HOUSES
ATSUGEWI (Hokan)	Lived on three streams that drained northward into Pit River.		About the same
YANA (Hokan)	Pit River and on edge of Sacramento Valley. Landmark in area was Mt. Lassen.		Earth-covered house.
YAHI (Hokan)	Mill and Deer Creeks that run into Sacramento River.		Lived part of the time in caves.
KAROK "upstream" (Hokan)	Three clusters of towns at mouths of Camp Creek, Salmon River, and Clear Creek. Along other parts of river were smaller villages.		
CHIMARIKO (Hokan)	Along twenty-mile stretch of Trinity River from mouth of South Fork to French Creek.		Houses had walls of bark, not planks.
SHASTAN (Hokan)	Klamath River, on Scott River and Shasta River. Limits formed by watershed that separates Sacramento, Trinity, and Salmon River from Mt. Shasta to Oregon mountains.	Made more use of skins because they lived in colder climate. Women wore hair in two wrapped clubs, "Yurok style."	
YUMA (Hokan)	Mostly the western bank of Colorado River and to mouth of Gila River.		

FOOD	BASKETS	BOATS	CUSTOMS AND OTHER INFORMATION
as the Achomawi.			Lived just south of the Achomawi
			Best warriors in the area; much feared by their neighbors. Had native dog much like coyote and used it for hunting. Tribe was very plain in its living.
			They were like their neighbors (Yurok) in almost everything. Never saw a white man until Gold Rush days. Had many ceremonies, at the beginning of each season especially. Had Girls' Ceremony also.
		River too small and rough for canoes, so they waded or swam across streams.	Poorer than the Yurok and Hupa. One of small tribes and miners may have killed most of them.
Mixed dry, powdered berries with meal to sweeten it. Pine nuts steamed, dried, and stored for winter.	Made few and so traded to get them.		Traded with the Kurok. Received dentalia shells, baskets, acorns. Gave deerskins, obsidian. Families made and owned own dams. Chief was head of richest family. No dancing except for war or to give shaman power to cure illness.
			Mourning ceremony for chiefs only. Both the Yuma and Mohave were warlike. Unlike any other tribes they used a shield when at war. Unlike all other California tribes, Yuma tribe learned how to farm and irrigate crops.

TRIBE (Family)	TERRITORY	CLOTHES AND ORNAMENTS	HOUSES
WASHO (Hokan)	Upper drainage of Truckee and Carson Rivers. Lake Tahoe in center of their territory.		Dome-shaped houses thatched with tule, leaves, or bark.
ESSELEN (Hokan)	Near part of Carmel River and rocky coast for twenty-five miles from near Point Sur to Point López.		
SALINAN (Hokan)	Near Santa Margarita Divide, north to Santa Lucia Peak, and somewhere south of Soledad.		
CHUMASH (Hokan)	Along Pacific Coast from Malibu Canyon to Point Concepcion and northward to Estero Bay.		Records show that some of their houses were very large—for as many as fifty people. Used mat curtains between rooms. Had raised beds.
POMO (Hokan)	Valley of the Russian River and all canyons of Coast Ranges. Its territory was coast, Russian River Valley, and Clear Lake district.	Skirts were of inner redwood bark fibers and tule grass. Sandals and leggings of tule; some of netted string. Men wore ear tubes made of bird bones or wooden rods tipped with feathers.	Homes along lakes in summer and along streams in winter. Loved to live in sunny places. Houses were redwood bark and cone-shaped, thatched with bundles of grass.

FOOD	BASKETS	BOATS	CUSTOMS AND OTHER INFORMATION
	Coiled baskets. Noted for excellent finish and design.		They were known as "Basin People."
			Smallest of all tribes and first to disappear. Probably lived in other places in the beginning and were pushed into a corner. Very little known about them.
			Traded and visited freely with the Yokuts. The Costonoans to the north were their enemies.
	Twined baskets, finely woven; some with small necks. Sealed with asphalt and used for water.	Had finest boats in California or any other place in the United States at that time. Their next-door neighbors, the Salinans, had none.	Had many large villages. Had charmstones that were highly prized. Once they were a very important group. Went to sea more than any other tribe. Had spears for catching sea otters and seals.
cean gave them mussels, surf fish, and sea ons. In winter the salmon ran upstream in vers and creeks and as plentiful. Small ame all year. Everyhere in their area ere was plenty of ood of all kinds.	No basket caps; used broad band on head. Their twined baskets called the finest baskets made in the world. Their coiled baskets used for gifts and trading. Made great use of tiny bright feathers and beads. Most tribes made about thirty wrappings an inch; the Pomo made sixty or more. Made sitting-up cradles.	Tule rush canoes on lakes. Coast people used redwood logs along shore but had no real boats.	One of best-known groups in California. Many villages—seventy-five large ones and almost five hundred smaller ones. Chief lived in largest village. Pomo owned salt beds and traded salt for goods from other tribes. Some of Pomo tribe still left. Had large earth-covered "dancing houses." Pomo were bankers of central California and made lots of shell money. Their tubular beads of magnesite were most prized, called "their gold." Had two kinds of chiefs: Great and Lesser Chiefs.

TRIBE (Family)	TERRITORY	CLOTHES AND ORNAMENTS	HOUSES
DIEGUEÑO "southerners" (Hokan)	Bordered by the Pacific Ocean and on the west by the Luiseño, Cupeño, and Cahuilla on the north (San Diego area). It is believed that the Kamia lived in the Imperial Valley but little is known about this.		House earth-covered. Three posts in row, log across top, poles leaned from the side. Covered with brush, then earth. Tent-shaped, unlike most other tribes.
MOHAVE (Hokan)	Southeast corner of state, on Colorado River.	Believed in tattooing and painting of faces more than other groups. Shells used more as ornaments than money. Loved all kinds of beads. Would trade almost anything to get beads.	Frame of poles, thatched and covered with sand. Men put large sleeping houses for themselves.
WINTUN (Penutian)	West side of Sacramento Valley from Sacramento River up to crest of Coast Range, Suisun, and San Pablo Bay, Napa and perhaps part of Sonoma Valley.		
MAIDU (Penutian)	Feather and American River from Sacramento River east to crest of Sierra Nevada Mts.		Bed was raised from floor. Pine needles used to make it soft. Many water birds in area and so blankets made of feathers.

FOOD	BASKETS	BOATS	CUSTOMS AND OTHER INFORMATION
	Made some pottery. In addition to baskets they made close-twined sacks or wallets of milkweed fiber. String colored red or white. Burden nets made of yucca fiber.		Not friendly to those at Mission San Diego; attacked, burned, and killed mission priest, the only priest who met death at hand of Indians in the history of the missions.
Planted beans, wheat, pumpkins, water-melons, cantaloupes.	Made coiled pottery but very poor baskets.		Fought tribes hundreds of miles away (as far as Chumash and Yokuts territories). Were friends with the Chemeheuvi because they let them pass through their area on way to war against other tribes. Used heavy clubs more than bows and arrows. The Mohave were tall, large-boned, and thin. Had a yellowish skin color and tied up their hair with clay. Either worked very hard or were lazy. They laughed freely and were not shy. They thought that every dream would come true. They had few ceremonies. Normal pace when traveling was a trot.
			Largest group in northern half of California. Had many kinds of dances (most important was Ghost Dance). Had men's secret society, the Kuksu.
Salmon, eels, eggs of yellow jackets, insects, grasshoppers were eaten. Bones were pounded and eaten raw.	Coiled baskets. Used willow and unpeeled redbud. Twined baskets for traps.	Used log rafts and flat dugout canoes and also tule. Usually tribes had one or the other; Maidu had both.	Often burned down trees to make "open country." They counted shell money by 10's, not by length of string. For fishing, had net on end of pole. Also had secret Kuksu society.

TRIBE (Family)	TERRITORY	CLOTHES AND ORNAMENTS	HOUSES
YOKUTS (Penutian)	Whole San Joaquin Valley from mouth of San Joaquin River to foot of Tehachapi Pass; lower hills of Sierra Nevada from Fresno River south.		Had several kinds of houses: cone-shaped, round, oblong. The oblong had shade porch in front.
MIWOK (Penutian)	Long slope of Sierra Nevada Mts. looking out over the San Joaquin Valley, Marin County, and part of Sonoma Valley. Were Coast, Lake, and Plains Miwok.		
COSTONOANS "coast people" (Penutian)	San Francisco Bay area, south to Point Sur, on east to Mt. Diablo.	Wore rabbit-skin coat during day, and used it as blanket at night. Men put mud on bodies in cold mornings until sun warmed them.	
PAIUTE-NORTH (Shoshonean)	Northeast corner of the state.		
MONO "persons" (Shoshonean)	Partly in Great Basin, some in Sierra Nevada Mts. Eastern Mono lived along base of the mountains. Owens River flowed through territory.		
KAWAIISU (Shoshonean)	Home was once in the Tehachapi Mts. Pressed in by neighbors on all sides.		

FOOD	BASKETS	BOATS	CUSTOMS AND OTHER INFORMATION
	Special jar-like-shaped baskets. Quail feathers woven in along upper edge. They were called "Tulare bottlenecks." Some of hill tribes made crude pottery by pressing hole in lump of clay.		
	Feather-decorated baskets like the Pomo. Very high storage baskets. Branches around sides. Branches pulled aside and acorns rolled out.		Coast Miwok was tribe that met Sir Francis Drake. He spent five days repairing the *Golden Hind* in Bay now known as Drake's Bay. Indians here believed that white men were spirits returned from the dead and so welcomed them. Also had secret Kuksu society.
Mussels must have been the main food because so many shell-mounds found in the area.		Tule rafts used to cross San Francisco Bay.	Ocean front and bay land lined with shell deposits, second only to the Santa Barbara Islands. The tribe fought just for fun of fighting—more a game with them. Painted bodies red and wore feathers more than most tribes. Sometimes women joined in the battles with strange cries.
			Many lakes, swamps, salt basins. Not much is known about them. Not much like any other tribe in the state.
			Little known about them.

TRIBE (Family)	TERRITORY	CLOTHES AND ORNAMENTS	HOUSES
PANAMINT (or KOSO) (Shoshonean)			
CHEMEHUEVI (or SOUTH PAIUTE) (Shoshonean)	Mountain range south of Death Valley and stretching to about Riverside and Imperial Counties.		Simple overhead shelters for sun or rain.
TUBATULABAL (Shoshonean)	Area drained by the Kern River down as far as a point halfway between the forks of the river and Bakersfield.		
SERRANO (Shoshonean)	Along San Bernardino Mt. range and San Gabriel Mts. west to Mt. San Antonio. San Bernardino County, not quite to city of Riverside.		
GABRIELEÑO (Shoshonean)	Fertile lands of Los Angeles County, some of Sierra Madre range, half of Orange County, and two islands, Santa Catalina and San Clemente.		
CUPEÑO (Shoshonean)	Near hot springs of present-day Warner's Ranch.		

FOOD	BASKETS	BOATS	CUSTOMS AND OTHER INFORMATION
Had few acorns but pine nuts were important as were seeds. Used lots of mesquite beans and reed stalks. Tree yucca buds were roasted. Agave was roasted in the ground. Cactus used. Mountain sheep was their meat.			
	Made a few simple pottery articles and painted designs on them.		
			Used to visit the Yokuts; married some of them. Young eagles were caught, cared for, and set free after taking feathers. Birds, geese, and even young coyotes kept as pets.
			Included the Alliklik, Vanyune. All this Serrano group were known as "mountaineers."
			Richest Indians in the state at time of the missions. Named after Mission San Gabriel. Fernandeño of the same group named after Mission San Fernando. They liked thick shells for money. Had a war club that was a straight heavy stick. Used only *metates* for pounding. Yang-na lived in what is now the Los Angeles city area.
			Very small group. Later went to Pala.

TRIBE (Family)	TERRITORY	CLOTHES AND ORNAMENTS	HOUSES
JUANEÑO (Shoshonean)	Area in between the Gabrieleño and Luiseño.		
LUISEÑO (Shoshonean)	West of the divide that is south of Mt. San Jacinto.	Back skirt women wore was made of soft inner bark of willow or cottonwood tree. Front skirt made of fiber strings. Tattooing done with juice of berries.	Earth-covered planks, unlike their neighbors.
CAHUILLA (Shoshonean)	Inland basin between San Bernardino Range and one southward from Mt. San Jacinto. Palm Springs area. The Desert Cahuilla were near the Salton Sea.		Houses were square or oblong with mat roofs and walls plastered with mud.

FOOD	BASKETS	BOATS	CUSTOMS AND OTHER INFORMATION
			Named after Mission San Juan Capistrano. All ceremonies held outdoors. Ceremonies held in atmosphere of great respect. Audience could only whisper. No hunter could eat his own fish or game. Two went together so they could exchange. Those who did not do this would either die or have bad luck.
Used more seeds of all kinds than acorns. Not many roots eaten. Rats, snakes, squirrels eaten. Rabbits cooked in earth oven or over open fire.	Made clay pots by coiling.	Had pine dugout canoes.	Outdoor ceremonial grounds. Had two entrances—one for dancers, one for others. Rest could look in from outside. Did not believe in sacred animals but in a God who helped them daily. Had a fire dance and stamped out fire with feet. Thought that all dead became stars and so named the stars. Named after Mission San Luis Rey.
In addition to other food, cactus was used. Fruits and fleshy leaves eaten. They used over sixty varieties of plants. Their seed-beaters were more important than a digging stick.	Made clay-coiled pots; also crudely woven seed-beaters.		One of most important tribes today in California. The government has brought water to area. Indians' rights are protected. They live in area they always have and their land is now very valuable.

INDEX

PICTOGRAPH FOUND IN A CAVE IN THE CHUMASH AREA
photo by Campbell Grant

PROPERTY
TOWN OF OXFORD

DATE DUE

Feb 3 '69			
SEP 29 '69			
NOV 14 '69			
DEC 15 '69			
MAY 11 '72			
MAY 26 '72			
OCT 2 '72			
MAR 5 74			
MAR 20 74			
MAY 11 '79			
MAY 21 '84			

970.4   **Bauer, Helen**
B   California Indian days

Oxford Middle School Library

A detailed picture of the life of the California Indians from earliest times to the present. Photographs and linecuts help to describe the history and culture of the tribes. Appendices of tribal names, pronunciation, location, habits and customs of the tribes summarize the text.

B 4-596